D1295152

WITCHCRAFT FOR DAILY SELF-CARE

WITCHCRAFT FOR DAILY SELF-CARE

NOURISHING RITUALS & SPELLS FOR A MORE BALANCED LIFE

MICHAEL HERKES

ILLUSTRATIONS BY BÁRBARA MALAGOLI

ROCKRIDGE
PRESS

Copyright © 2021 by Rockridge Press

All rights reserved. No part of this publication may be reproduced, stored in a retrieval system, or transmitted in any form or by any means, electronic, mechanical, photocopying, recording, scanning, or otherwise without the prior written permission of the Publisher. Requests to the Publisher for permission should be addressed to the Permissions Department, Rockridge Press, 1955 Broadway, Suite 400, Oakland, CA 94612.

First Rockridge Press hardcover edition 2022

Originally published in trade paperback by Rockridge Press 2021

Rockridge Press and the Rockridge Press logo are trademarks or registered trademarks of Callisto Media Inc. and/or its affiliates in the United States and other countries and may not be used without written permission.

For general information on our other products and services, please contact our Customer Care Department within the United States at (866) 744-2665, or outside the United States at (510) 253-0500.

Hardcover ISBN: 979-8-88608-423-8 | Paperback ISBN: 978-1-64876-912-2
eBook ISBN: 978-1-64876-913-9

Manufactured in the United States of America

Interior and Cover Designer: Angela Navarra
Art Producer: Hannah Dickerson
Editor: Sean Newcott
Production Editor: Nora Milman
Production Manager: Holly Haydash

Illustrations © Bárbara Malagoli, 2021

10 9 8 7 6 5 4 3 2 1 0

This book is dedicated to my continued
relationship with self-care.

CONTENTS

INTRODUCTION

Dear Reader,

Hello there! Welcome to *Witchcraft for Daily Self-Care*. My name is Michael and I have been a practicing witch for more than 20 years. During those two decades, I have practiced my witchery alone, building a unique personal practice as a devotee of Lilith, the rebel goddess of witchcraft, equality, sensuality, and self-care. Four years ago, however, I decided to step out from the shadows of my solitary witch world and step into the role of teacher of the craft. I chose to dedicate my energy to uplifting and mentoring others on using witchcraft for self-empowerment. Since then, I've written a variety of articles and books, presented workshops across the United States, and spoken on various podcasts. I've made a name for myself as "The Glam Witch"—known for a bubbly personality and eccentric flair for magical fashion. But underneath the fluff and puff of pink tulle, sequin kimonos, and glittery eye shadow lies a less glamorous world that includes anxiety, depression, doubt, pressure, and trauma that pop up like whack-a-moles on a regular basis while I try to live my best life.

I started practicing witchcraft during a traumatic, hellish time in junior high. Plagued by fear, self-loathing, and loneliness, I manifested a teenage idolization for self-masochistic defeat. I became my own worst enemy while trying to tackle the pressures of life and society. As I've evolved, I've experienced some pretty dark times, as I am sure you have, too. These have included traumatic childhood encounters, deaths, physical assault, mental abuse, gut-wrenching breakups, daunting deadlines, and other anxiety-driven pressures. Despite all this, I found a way to courageously walk down a unique path—one that helped me pick up the sword and slay the demons of my life one by one. That path is witchcraft, and the sword is self-care.

We are living in troubled times. Our environment is increasingly challenged, freedoms are being stripped away, and we are navigating life through a global pandemic. Meanwhile, we still have our daily responsibilities to uphold. Sometimes life can feel as though it is unraveling at the seams. Witchcraft calls upon us to use the power of self-care to heal ourselves so that we can beam with big witch energy. And it is from this perspective that I want to share with you the secret to how I've been able to cultivate happiness, even in the darkest of days.

This book is a guide to establishing a daily routine of self-care anchored in the practice of witchcraft. Part 1 explores how witchcraft and self-care intertwine to improve your life. I'll cover the fundamental knowledge needed to approach the spells and rituals of the book with confidence and ease. Part 2 of the book walks you through 90 days of healing spells, rituals, and remedies all centered around mind, body, spirit, environment, relationships, and personal success. These spells and rituals build off one another and are designed to be followed in order. However, feel free to jump around based on your intuition, expertise, or desired self-care for the moment. Whether you are new to witchcraft or a seasoned practitioner looking for new inspiration, this book is designed to help you tap into your pure potential with magic and summon the self-care needed for a radically new, magical you.

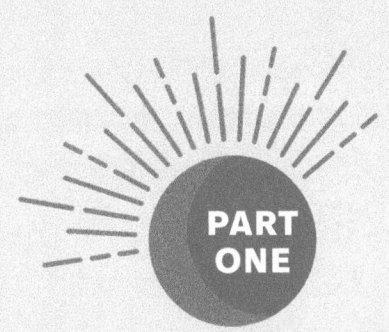

WITCHCRAFT
FOR
SELF-CARE

Welcome to part 1 of *Witchcraft for Daily Self-Care*! To start your journey, this section provides an overview of witchcraft, self-care, and how the two intentionally and magically intersect. It's also specifically designed to establish a foundation for the newest practitioners of witchcraft but can also serve as a great refresher for anyone who has been practicing for years. Think of part 1 as a primer for the 90 days of exercises, spells, and rituals that you will encounter in part 2. There's much magic to look forward to and self-care to foster, so let's begin.

CHAPTER ONE

UNDERSTANDING WITCHCRAFT AND MAGIC

Year after year, new articles are written highlighting the ever-increasing interest in witchcraft. The social media world is riddled with the witch aesthetic—whether it's astrology, crystals, or tarot cards—and serves endless audiences with mass enchantment. But witchcraft is so much more than a trend or fashion statement. It is an empowering spiritual practice that centers around the intention of will, esoteric enlightenment, and personal empowerment, making it a wonderful tool for establishing self-care. Let's take this chapter to explore the wonderful world of witchcraft and all it has to offer your daily life.

WHAT IS WITCHCRAFT?

Witchcraft is an exotic word that often brings a handful of classic images to mind. Some think of witches as demonic child-stealing hags whose idea of a happy meal is the child itself, or they may think of a bewitching sorceress like *The Love Witch*'s Elaine Parks or even a rebellious teenager like Sabrina, tackling "chilling adventures." As modern witchcraft evolves over time, it is becoming tougher to define what a witch is. Modern witchcraft practitioners are a diverse and creative group of individuals who tap into the unseen forces of the universe and manifest their best lives.

At its core, witchcraft *is* the practice of magic. Not the glittery, flame-throwing, green potions and flying on broomsticks kind of magic, but the magic of creating change with will. Witchcraft is in fact a craft—something that is made in the same manner that an artist would create art. Instead of using a canvas, paint, brushes, and other mediums, witches use a variety of sources to manipulate energy with intention. Energy sources are the ingredients to a witch's working and include crystals, colors, herbs, oils, timings, and other artifacts that are molded together into the art of magic.

MAKING MAGIC

How many times have you made a wish while blowing out your birthday candles, created a vision board, dressed in a "power" outfit, or picked a penny off the street? Or maybe you've made your family's amazing chicken noodle soup while thinking about how much it will help you recover from a cold. Although these actions may seem like nothing more than clichés or superstitions, they are actually variations of magic spells used by modern witches.

Although there are a number of diverse traditions and branches of practice in the magical community, all use intention to create change in the world. Regardless of the end goal, spells are essentially a witch's version of a prayer and are ultimately the language of magic. They combine the power of intention, the spoken word, natural ingredients, and the laws of attraction to result in manifestation.

Your magic and spellcraft can be as simple or complex as you'd like. The beauty of the world of witchcraft is its diversity. This is one reason why not all witches practice the same kind of magic. We all have our own interests, talents, and destinies, which impact how we express our magical currents. This is why many solitary witches are considered eclectic—pulling from a variety of different types of magic.

TYPES OF MAGIC

There are many different ways to practice magic, and part 2 of this book explores several magical niches. Therefore, let's take a moment to briefly go over the different forms of magical expression that you'll encounter.

Cooking Magic is the skill of infusing the culinary arts with intention. Kitchen witches are skilled in cooking up potions like teas, elixirs, and cocktails, as well as other treats and feasts fueled by a magical goal or healing need. These edible forms of alchemy are brewed using the metaphysical energies of the herbs and ingredients to produce the practitioner's desired outcome.

Divination Magic centers around using the power of tools such as tarot or oracle cards, crystal scrying, tea leaves, or pendulums to heighten intuition, predict natural events, or delve deeper into understanding one's self.

Glamour Magic is associated with attraction, beauty, love, and enchantment. It is a visual form of magic that bewitches onlookers with the alluring aesthetic. This form of magic is made by using fashion, makeup, beauty products, and other forms of visual representation to create the desired change. The primary reason to use this type of magic is to attract friendship, love, jobs, or general success and attention.

Natural Magic uses the natural world to enhance spellcasting. Practitioners who focus their efforts on this form of magic are generally referred to as green witches because of their green thumbs. They are experts in conjuring the energy of the terrestrial realm including herbs, plants, crystals, and animals.

Planetary Magic is associated with the magic of the celestial realms. Witches who work with this magic focus heavily on astrology, the phases of the moon, and other planetary phenomena to enhance their spellwork.

Ritual Magic often includes dramatic rituals and incantations to conjure spirits, deities, and other forms of energy. It is highly influenced by the rich and varied tradition of occultism and commonly includes repetitive themes, gestures, and movements.

Sex Magic uses sensuality as a form of magical fruition. Witches who practice this type of magic harness energy through their orgasms.

MAGIC MISNOMERS

Both history and Hollywood have done their fair share of creating magical myths that are divorced from reality. When it comes to the superstitions surrounding witchcraft and magical practices, here are some concepts that don't add up to our real ways.

Witches can only be cis-women. Although more women than men are practitioners, witchcraft welcomes all genders and identities, the same way that it is inclusive of race, sexual orientation, and any other distinguishers. Hollywood has stereotyped male magic makers as warlocks, but historically, the word "warlock" has meant "oath-breaker," leaving many male witches to shy away from this label. There are many different titles and terms for people in the magical community. As a general rule, it is important to never make assumptions and always ask others about what term they identify with.

Witches are evil and worship the devil. In short, the devil is a Christian concept that has nothing to do with our magical practices. Many witches worship different deities from ancient civilizations. Although there is a general emphasis on goddess worship, male deities are included in some practices. During the rise of Christianity, horned deities became scapegoats for the dominating patriarchy as symbols of negativity and evil. In truth, deities like Pan and Cernunnos are benevolent gods who rule over nature, hunting, and sexuality.

You must belong to a coven to be a witch. There is something truly magical about having a squad of fellow witches to summon up empowerment and rejoice in magic together. However, solitary practice is a valid, powerful, and popular method of practicing witchcraft.

You have to practice the same as everyone else. The art of witchcraft offers a kaleidoscope of color. When I first started my practice, I felt that I needed every tool and had to be a master of all the different magical types. Comparison is deadly and can wreak havoc on our self-care. The reality is that we are all drawn to different things and should explore them freely.

It's *only* about intention. Although intentions do help in fueling magic, they are only one ingredient in the grand scheme of our workings. There are no shortcuts for learning the hows and whys of witchcraft. Also, anything magical must also be followed up with practical actions in the mundane world. If you want a new job, you must actually apply for one in addition to doing spellwork. Want to win the lottery? Play it! Desire a new love? Put yourself out there! Manifestations must be followed up with real-life efforts.

It's all love and light. This phrase has spread quicker than wildfire around many spiritual communities. Although the idea of a land filled with love and light sounds wonderful, light can blind us to truth and keep us from growth. Witches work with nature, and nature is both light and dark. Dark does not mean bad or evil; it is from the dark phases of life that we can grow, evolve, and change.

THE HEALING POWER OF NATURE AND WITCHCRAFT

Witches have long been connected to nature and the art of healing. Our roots extend from ancient pagan practices, when the people had a close connection to the land and worked as healers by harnessing the power of nature. Just as they understood then, witches today know that we need nature to survive. Likewise, nature is a sacred space that we should work to preserve. Not only is Earth *our* home, but it is the one and only home for other species and creatures that assist in our well-being. Many plants, animals, and earthbound substances contribute to the healing of ailments, stress, and other conditions. Simply walking in nature and experiencing the fresh air can elevate your mood and dissolve stress. All the natural world around us offers inspiration and understanding that can heal.

Nature is the map to a witch's magical journey. The ingredients to our spellcasting all derive from nature. Everything from crystals to plants, seasons to moon phases, come as expressions of the natural world. Many witches also partake in alternative health practices such as yoga, Reiki, and herbalism, which harness the power of nature.

Nature teaches us that there has to be dark to see the light. From the death of winter, we experience rebirth in the spring. Everything in nature is temporary and yet creates a continuous cycle of life, death, and rebirth. Therefore, witches honor the darkness as the pivotal place where transformation is created and self-empowerment is found.

FIVE MINUTES IN NATURE

I make an effort every day to go outside for a few minutes. When I do, I notice that my entire mood shifts, and I feel better. A bit of fresh air, chirping birds, and the sight of blooming flora can instantly shake me from whatever burdens I am carrying and instill in me a deeper appreciation for the moment. It has even been scientifically proven that being in nature can have a profound impact on physical and emotional well-being. Nature helps heal us from the inside out.

HOW WITCHCRAFT EMBRACES SELF-CARE

Witchcraft is the tool that allows you to be the conductor of the symphony of magic that is your life. A major aspect of being a witch involves working with the inner parts of ourselves and our intuition. Our magic is an extension of our being, which is why it intersects perfectly with self-care. By tapping into the healing nature of witchcraft through self-reflection, creativity, and mindfulness, we can actively engage in the magical maintenance of the self. Witchcraft embraces self-care in two distinct areas: for the individual and for the world at large.

FOR THE INDIVIDUAL

In many ways, witchcraft is about power—but not power over others. Instead, witchcraft helps build personal empowerment. Much of this is because it places a huge amount of emphasis on identity and self-discovery, while also allowing for the creative flow of imagination. Both witchcraft and self-care put an emphasis on healing ourselves so that we can be better in the world.

FOR THE BROADER WORLD

Witches are connected to the natural world around us in a deeper and more profound way than most. Witchcraft not only helps instill a deeper connection to nature, but also to society and our general environment. It is from this deep respect for our planet that we work toward being of service to it and all its inhabitants. It is for this reason that much of today's witchcraft is linked to environmentalism, feminism, and political resistance. To be of service to the world around us, we have to ensure that we ourselves are prepared to do so, making self-care an essential component to a witch's success.

WHAT CAN WITCHCRAFT TEACH US ABOUT CARING FOR OURSELVES?

Witchcraft teaches us how to tap into our own inner world and experience it through the natural order of life. It is much more than the fluff and sparkle of an Instagram filter. Even while demonstrating my glittery femme-forward, pink-loving witch aesthetic, there is seriousness to my practice. It is a deep, spiritual discipline, not a temporary fix for life's problems. It is designed to help us evolve, come into our personal power, and be of service to the world around us.

To be of service, we must work on ourselves first. We are conduits for the power of magic. If our drains are clogged with muck and gunk, our magic cannot flow freely. Being a practitioner of witchcraft requires awareness of ourselves and our actions so that we can better care for ourselves.

PRIORITIZING OURSELVES AND OUR DREAMS

We truly live in a magical world. However, the most magical world we will ever know is the one that is *within* us. Tapping into our own creative expression and allowing it to flow freely is one small step in prioritizing ourselves and our dreams. Growing up, I was told that I could be anything I wanted to be. There is much truth in that. If we believe in ourselves and allow the universe to have a little bit of say, magical things happen.

SETTING INTENTIONS

Our emotions amplify our magic. If we are constantly living in a state of fear, shame, or pain, we are only going to experience more of that. That is not to say that these emotions won't surface from time to time or that they are not valid. They are part of our inner natures. That said, like attracts like. We can be emotionally intentional about what we want to attract. Set your intentions wisely and purposefully.

ACCOUNTABILITY FOR ACTION

It's not *just* about our wants, desires, and intentions. It is also by *doing* that we make magic come to life. Magic must be followed up with real-world action. Therefore, witchcraft holds us accountable for manifesting our dreams practically and magically.

DRAWING POWER FROM THE WORLD AROUND US

We all need a bit of inspiration every now and then, and the world around us offers a never-ending reservoir. Because witches are tapped into nature on a higher frequency than most, our eyes are open to experiencing the world around us in a deeper way, allowing us to find inspiration in nature, technology, movies, reality, and all the realms in between to bloom into the best version of ourselves.

HEALING OURSELVES FIRST

There is a reason why flight attendants review the instructions for what to do in an emergency before takeoff. In all cases, it is essential to take care of ourselves before assisting others. The same goes for magical self-care. Healing ourselves first allows us to be fully charged, functional, and ready to navigate any problems we may encounter. When we take the time to work on ourselves, we are more useful to others as well.

MAGICAL MINDFULNESS

Mindfulness is an essential element to magic and self-care. This is because it helps focus our attention inward to establish a deeper connection to the now. Mindfulness is found in a variety of spiritual practices as a way to disengage with preoccupations and cultivate a stronger appreciation for life. It also helps reduce stress, combat anxiety, and enhance self-awareness. Three techniques used to practice mindfulness are breathing exercises, meditation, and visualization.

Breathing exercises are one of the best ways to manage stress and also help put your body in a state that is conducive to performing rituals and spellcasting. Box breathing is a technique that involves slowly inhaling through your nose and exhaling through your mouth, holding each for four seconds. This can be done for as few as five minutes to help promote an overall sense of calmness.

Meditation allows thoughts to come and go organically, allowing the brain to rest and rejuvenate while creating a sense of relaxation. This can be done by simply closing your eyes and letting your mind wander for a few minutes.

Visualizing our ideas or intentions helps manifest them, which is why it is always important to have a clear vision of how you want your goals to manifest. Visualizations are best achieved when coupled with meditation. Visualize a scene or scenario such as meeting a spirit guide in a cave, or actions such as getting promoted, mending a friendship, etc.

TRUSTING OUR INNER WITCH

Have you ever had a gut feeling? Maybe something telling you to take or not take a specific action? Perhaps it was a little voice guiding you through a situation or a feeling causing you to react in a specific way. These are examples of how intuition can guide us. For me, it took a while to learn how to trust my intuition. I spent many years ignoring it altogether only to get hurt later on. I got tired of looking in the mirror and saying, "I told you so," so I changed gears and finally started to listen to my inner voice. Intuition is a witch's greatest tool, guiding us through the darkest of times and honoring our needs. It can keep us balanced and let us know when to press pause or go a different direction.

CONCLUSION

Witchcraft is a spiritual practice that many have turned to for self-empowerment. At their core, witches are healers who pull from the natural world for magic, but true magic starts within. Therefore, it is essential to focus on self-care. We'll learn more about this in the next chapter.

CHAPTER TWO

THE SOOTHING POWER OF SELF-CARE

S elf-care is more than a millennial trend or hashtag on social media. The ancient Greeks believed that to care for others, we must first take care of ourselves. "Philautia" was the Greek word that translated to "self-care" or "self-love." The Greek philosopher Aristotle wrote of this love by exclaiming, "All friendly feelings for others are an extension of man's feelings for himself." In many ways, people today have turned to self-care as a form of self-improvement, yet there can be a misconception that practicing self-care is selfish. This chapter is devoted to exploring the soothing power that self-care has to offer, fostering positivity, and discovering methods for integrating self-care daily.

DEFINING SELF-CARE

Just like witchcraft, talk of self-care seems to be everywhere these days. And as with witchcraft, it is a very personal practice that differs from person to person. To some of us, it is a warm bubble bath with rose petals, a bottle of wine, an indulgent meal, or a vacation. But at its core, self-care is less about the material means of modern luxury and more about the actions and the conscious effort to care for ourselves. These actions can be taking 15 to 30 minutes of the day to meditate, saying "no" when we have reached our capacity of doing for others, or creating boundaries to protect our personal needs.

THE BENEFITS OF SELF-CARE

Think back to a time when you did not feel completely yourself. Stressful and negative situations are a part of life. Sometimes they are short-lived and other times it takes a while to pick ourselves back up. Regardless, we are better equipped to navigate the obstacles of life when our personal needs are taken care of. Self-care is known for its ability to combat situations like stress, anxiety, and depression while also helping us sleep better, focus more, and have a stronger appreciation for life.

HEALING OUR MINDS, BODIES, AND SPIRITS

Since I started dabbling in the world of witchery, I've heard of the "mind, body, and spirit" used as a magical trinity in reference to our mental, physical, and spiritual health. A healthy mind is achieved by balancing mental stimulation and rest. Exercising our brains regularly can help reduce tension and stress, allowing us to experience more joy. A healthy body is necessary for energy and to help fight against illnesses and ailments. Proper nutrition and exercise help keep the body physically well. A healthy spirit allows for free-flowing inspiration and creativity and can also shape our morals, ethics, and overall way of life. Self-care nourishes all these components.

INCREASING OUR SELF-LOVE
AND SELF-APPRECIATION

Self-love is not a narcissistic, ego-driven attitude that you are better than everyone else. Instead, it is the conscious act of treating ourselves with respect despite our flaws and forgiving our failures. It helps facilitate compassion and allows us to be the most authentic versions of ourselves, free of shame, guilt, and even loneliness. When you are your own best friend, you allow the real you to be seen, and you set a standard for how to treat and interact with others, positioning yourself to form meaningful relationships.

GIVING OURSELVES ROOM TO
THINK AND BREATHE

We live in an action-oriented world, and I personally used to struggle with pressing pause. However, I have learned that it is from hiatus that we can truly recharge. Like a car, we need fuel to move and do what we're meant to do. Continuously living on empty is unsustainable. Self-care gives us permission to take a time-out, reflect, and refocus our energy to move forward with a well-balanced, happy life.

CULTIVATING A POSITIVE OUTLOOK

Being positive is not the same as burying our heads in the sand and ignoring life's burdens. However, self-care can help us foster a positive outlook, which allows us to see the glass as being half-full rather than half-empty. This approach to living helps us deal with unpleasantness in a more productive and proactive manner. When we understand our needs and make realistic efforts to tender them, we can develop optimism.

PRIORITIZING OUR GOALS AND DREAMS

Too often, we put our goals and dreams on hold to do what others expect of us. Sometimes current circumstances might seem so restrictive that it feels easier to put our goals on the back burner and procrastinate our happiness. But when we anchor our goals in something about which we are truly passionate, there is always a strong chance of success. Self-care encourages us to actively engage in our dreams to make them a reality. By employing self-care techniques, we are also more likely to be inspired and think of creative ways to overcome obstacles.

CHANGING HOW WE SHOW UP IN THE WORLD

By taking the steps to become the biggest and brightest expression of ourselves, we are bound to attract more greatness. Radiating with confidence and positivity lets us grab life by the reins and become an active participant in shaping our destiny. Being fully fueled allows us to be better contributors not just to our lives, but to the world around us. Remember that witchcraft encourages being of service, and when we jive to the rhythm of our souls, we can better engage with our relationships, communities, and environment.

OVERCOMING SELF-CARE STUMBLES

One of the reasons why self-care attempts can fail is because of unrealistic expectations about the process. Self-care is not an event that takes place one day and then—*poof!*—you are done and good to go. It is a transformative practice that progresses over time. The same can be said for witchcraft.

But it is not just about setting realistic expectations and sticking to the process. We also have to take self-care seriously to benefit from it. Yes, we all have a variety of responsibilities and it can be oh so challenging to put them on hold. But that mindset won't get us anywhere. Seriously planning for self-care and sticking to it is a huge first step.

We should never feel guilty about putting ourselves and our needs first. Release guilt and surrender the idea that self-care is selfish. These negative feelings will only hold us back. However, we must also be mindful not to fall into any self-care traps. It is important not to develop an excessive lenience for engaging in vices that are counterproductive to our well-being.

INTENTIONS AND MANIFESTATION

When it comes to spellcasting, the most powerful part is the intent. The more passion we pour into our spells, the more they will be able to manifest. For this reason, it is very important to have a clear vision in mind when determining what it is we plan on witchcrafting. But remember—manifesting is not an instant occurrence, nor should it be a quick fix to a problem. Manifestation and the magic of spellcasting happen when we visualize our goals and deliberately make the efforts to go after them in the real world. To achieve magically, we must do practically.

WITCHCRAFTING SELF-CARE FOR ALL PARTS OF LIFE

Witchcraft is a powerful tool to help us evolve into our best selves. As we engage in self-care activities, we cultivate confidence in our lives and our craft. The more self-assured we are and the more we courageously trust our intuition, the more successful our magic will be.

MIND

Our thoughts create our realities, and we should be careful about what we put into the universe. Stress and negativity can adversely affect the magic that we are conjuring, so our magical minds should be powered by positivity. In this way, magic helps the mind by offering empowerment, flexing our imaginations to transcend our current situations and reach our higher selves. Likewise, reflection can assist in overcoming anger and sadness and lead us to forgiveness.

BODY

Our bodies are the outer shells of our souls. The body is the machine that drives our magic. Self-care of our bodies amplifies our energy and allows us to embrace the magic of our physical form. Combining nutrition and other science-based knowledge of herbs with their magical correspondences promotes overall health, external beauty, and restful sleep. Witchcraft for our bodies includes activities such as eating with intention, crafting restorative potions that heal us, and grooming to promote desired presentation.

SPIRIT

Spirit transcends the physical plane. It is not of the body or mind, but rather the spiritual ether that connects us to our ancestors, deities, and our own inner divinity. An important aspect of self-care is determining our identities and searching for the meaning of life. Including spiritual consideration in our self-care rituals can help us live our best lives.

ENVIRONMENT

Our environment starts with where we live and is the platform our self-care is built on. The home is more than a shelter; it should be a space where we feel safe to be whoever we are. It should be a socket we can plug into for rejuvenation and self-healing. Still, the environment is also the abundant space outside our homes, helping us connect with the natural forces of magic and proactively assist us in preserving nature.

SELF-CARE AND SHADOW WORK

An essential theme of self-care and witchcraft is shadow work. The shadow is an unknown side to our personalities—that which the conscious ego rejects. It encompasses personality traits that we have suppressed, pushed away, and ignored, often as a result of the negative consequences associated with them. There is a misconception that the shadow is bad and that the light is good. It is okay to feel sad, angry, hurt, and upset from time to time. The key component to shadow work is identifying what traits are a part of our shadows and finding ways to productively integrate them into our consciousness. By doing so, we have a better understanding of ourselves.

RELATIONSHIPS AND COMMUNITY

People are communal creatures. We crave companionship, whether that is from friendship, romance, family, or community. This is the level of self-care that extends into creating harmony and unity through togetherness. By understanding our needs and making them a priority, we can better engage in attracting others to us and set the bar for how we will interact with and treat others.

PROSPERITY AND SUCCESS

When we are deeply in touch with ourselves, owning who we are and loving every part of it, we start to become a magnet for more great things, including an abundance of success. Being in tune with our individual magic allows us to set goals, act in confidence, and find prosperity in all areas of life.

IDENTIFYING OUR SELF-CARE GOALS

Are you ready to lean into daily self-care that is anchored in the mysterious practice of witchcraft? Before we get started, we should ask ourselves what our self-care goals are. Identifying these will better assist us in setting intentions and manifesting magic. The following are five recommended steps for determining and reaching our self-care goals:

1. **SELF-ASSESSMENT**

   When it comes to magical self-care, we must first start by determining what it is that makes us happy. Take inventory of your happiness by creating a list of your favorite things and why they make you feel good.

2. PRIORITIZE

To be successful and summon magical self-care, we must make it a priority. There is only one way to make the time for self-care: Clear your plate. Sadly, we can't do it all, and cutting back on other activities is an essential part of self-care.

3. OWN IT

Self-care has been romanticized as being fluffy, pretty, and positive. However, to truly benefit from self-care, we have to prepare to be uncomfortable. There are going to be unpleasant feelings that surface while confronting our inner emotional landscape and prioritizing our needs over others'. Self-care is about navigating and balancing our shadow selves with our light halves.

4. ESTABLISH BOUNDARIES

A crucial part of establishing a daily self-care practice is establishing boundaries. These boundaries can be emotional or physical and essentially help keep us stable by determining what we are and are not comfortable with. Boundaries give us permission to disengage from uncomfortable situations that take away our energy and leave us feeling burnt out.

5. STOP PEOPLE-PLEASING

There is a big difference between being of service and being a doormat. We cannot allow the opinions of others and their ideas of who we should be to take precedence in our lives. People may always tell us that we can't do something or that something won't work. Stop listening to the naysayers and those who do not lift you up. Every day is an opportunity to learn, grow, and experience the adventures of our own lives for ourselves—not others.

STICKING WITH IT EVERY DAY

The secret to self-care is establishing a daily routine. It might seem challenging to prioritize daily self-care with all the other tasks we take on, but it is so important for our well-being. One of the best ways to stick with our daily self-care routines is to schedule them. This can be as simple as making sure we leave ourselves enough time to get adequate sleep, cook a meal, take a hot bath, or go to the gym. It can be a quick meditation during a lunch break, or an entire weekend away in the woods.

CONCLUSION

Self-care is an essential component to happiness and balance in our daily lives. When our needs are met, we are more capable of being productive and of service to others. Witchcraft is a spiritual tool that can be used to tend to our minds, bodies, and spirits and forge a deeper connection to our environment, communities, and personal successes. Now that we have examined what self-care is and how it intersects with witchcraft, let's look at some of the ingredients and practices we can use to summon self-care sorcery!

CHAPTER THREE

THE INGREDIENTS OF MAGICAL SELF-CARE

Witches use a lot of ingredients to amplify our intentions and bring our magic into existence. Similar to cooking a meal, we witches need to determine what ingredients are needed to whip up our feasts. Each ingredient has a different energy, and this chapter is devoted to exploring the different kinds of ingredients and magical tools we can use for self-care.

THE MAGIC OF THE
NATURAL WORLD

The natural world produces everything we need for magical self-care. Understanding how each part of nature is a piece of a greater magical system helps us develop a deeper connection to it. Nature is all around us—all the time. It is the air that we breathe, the ground we walk on, the flaming sun shining down on us, the water we drink, and the glittering tapestry of stars in the universe surrounding us.

THE ELEMENTS

The four elements—earth, air, fire, and water—are integral parts of the natural world and witchcraft. They are often part of ritual work and can be used to further manifest your self-care.

Earth, associated with the north, represents structure and form and helps ground our energies. Connect to earth energy when looking for stability. Spending time outside in nature, eating organic local produce, and decorating our spaces with plants, crystals, and other earthly objects can help us connect to this element.

Air, associated with the east, governs ideas, intellect, communication, and practicality. Connect with this element for inspiration or mental energy. The best way to connect with air is to do breathing exercises or spend time outside on a windy day. Wind chimes, bells, and feathers help manifest the element of air.

Fire, associated with the south, represents action, creativity, courage, passion, and transformation. This element is best connected with for anything that involves physical energy, creative passion, or strength in difficult situations. Physically, exercise and sexuality are prime representations of fire. We can connect physically with fire by lighting candles, exercising, or embracing our sensuality.

Water, associated with the west, stands for compassion, love, and forgiveness. Because it is connected to our emotions, it also has a deep undertone that resonates with our intuitive health and encourages us to trust our guts. We can connect to water to get in touch with our emotional health. Taking baths, swimming, stepping out in the rain, or observing natural bodies of water like oceans, lakes, rivers, or streams can help access the power of this element.

We all typically have an element that we connect with the most and the least. An important part of witchcraft and self-care is finding ways to be more balanced. Therefore, it is a good idea to surround ourselves more with the elements to which we feel least connected.

WHEEL OF THE YEAR

Traditional practices of witchcraft are known for celebrating the eight holidays known as Sabbats. These days correspond with major astrological and agricultural events; they celebrate and explore the cyclical flow of life, death, and rebirth. Understanding the seasons and acknowledging the Sabbats is a way to engage in magical self-care through symbolic transformation. The following is a chart of the Sabbats, their magical themes, and self-care practices for observation.

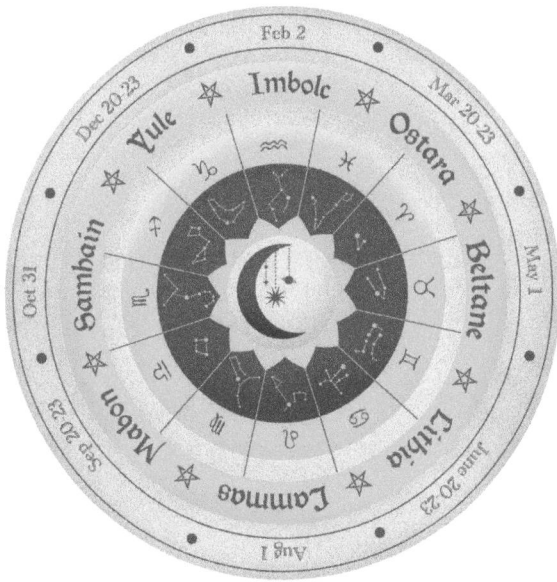

SABBAT	DATES	MAGICAL THEMES	SELF-CARE ACTIVITIES
Samhain (Halloween)	**October 31**	Transformation, passage, divination, observing magic and the supernatural; retreat into the quiet and cold time of the year	Practice divination for self, decorate graves of loved ones, build an altar, create a spell bottle for protection, or dress up as someone you admire for Halloween
Yule (Winter Solstice)	**December 20–23**	Hope, comfort, blessings, reflection, rest, and coziness	Spend time in pajamas at home, send holiday cards with encouraging and personal messages, make cookies with magical intentions, exchange handmade gifts with loved ones, or burn a Yule log in the fireplace
Imbolc (Candlemas)	**February 2**	Inspiration, creativity, purification, and meditation	Clean the home and donate excess, write poetry, take a purifying bath, meditate in candlelight, or practice restorative yoga
Ostara (Spring Equinox)	**March 20–23**	Growth, prosperity, fertility, and opportunity	Create a to-do list with goals to reach at the Sabbats through the remainder of the year, go for a hike and look for signs of nature returning, start a garden, or create a prosperity spell with seeds

SABBAT	DATES	MAGICAL THEMES	SELF-CARE ACTIVITIES
Beltane (May Eve)	**May 1**	Sensuality, love, instincts, and emergence	Create sex and love magic, enchant a perfume to attract romantic partners, go dancing, or join a drum circle
Litha (Summer Soltice)	**June 20–23**	Dreams, the fae, manifestation, and power	Leave offerings for the fae, do some dream magic, go swimming and envision healing, or go to a summer festival
Lughnasadh (Lammas)	**August 1**	Sacrifice, achievement, games, and fruition	Have a salad with locally sourced produce, try an active exercise routine, or do some banishment magic to remove things that no longer benefit you
Mabon (Autumn Equinox)	**September 20–23**	Harvest, gatherings, transition, and the veil beginning to thin	Host a dinner party with close friends, visit an apple orchard and observe the feeling of autumn, revisit your goal list from Ostara, or consider what you are thankful for

PHASES OF THE MOON

Deeply connected to intuition, magic, and the occult, the moon is often used as an energy source for spellcraft and as an expression of the divine feminine. Many witches hold lunar celebrations, known as esbats, at the new and/or full moon phases. Each of the eight phases of the moon holds metaphysical symbolism.

New moon: The first phase of the moon's cycle. Magically, this is a time to set intentions.

Waxing crescent: A sliver of silver light in the sky, reminiscent of a backward "C," and a time to focus on taking action.

First quarter: A time when the moon's appearance is 50 percent lit on the right side. It is a great time to determine what decisions need to be made to bring our magic to fruition.

Waxing gibbous: The ripe time just before the full phase. It is a source of abundant energy and allows us to get specific about our magical intentions.

Full moon: A time to glow and celebrate the bounty of lunar energy.

Waning gibbous: A time to express gratitude for all that we have received and for what we are asking for, even if it has not yet manifested.

Last quarter: A time when the moon is at 50 percent illumination on the left side. In this waning phase, the energies of the moon can be focused on forgiveness.

Waning crescent: The last phase and a time to offer release and surrender to what no longer serves us.

For a more in-depth look at moon magic, check out *The Complete Book of Moon Spells: Rituals, Practices, and Potions for Abundance* by yours truly!

FLOWERS, HERBS, AND RESINS

Plants provide beauty and nourishment and have been used in many cultures as a source of physical healing. But the plant kingdom offers much more than medicines for our physical ailments. Plants are also a spiritual medicine. Each plant has its own set of unique metaphysical properties. An important element of making magic is using our intuition to guide us in what to use. Be that as it may, not all plants (or other ingredients for that matter) work for the same types of magic. I have listed some of the more common herbs that we will be using in part 2 of the book in a chart on page 35, along with their corresponding purposes. If a spell calls for a specific herb that is not available, we can replace it with an ingredient that has the same energy.

When working with herbs, it is best to grow them ourselves. If purchasing herbs, it is best to stock a magical pantry with organic specimens that are reserved for spellcraft only.

PLANT ANATOMY

Another way to work magically with plants is to drill down into the anatomy of the plant itself. Just as different plants are used for different magical outcomes, different parts of the plant can be further broken down to assist with more specific types of spellwork.

Flowers represent attraction or repulsion.
Fruit or berries are used for culmination or reward.
Leaves provide nourishment.
Roots lend stability.
Seeds offer new beginnings.
Stems or branches represent growth and progress.
Thorns or bark are used for protection and banishment.

Let's look at roses, a popular ingredient for love magic, as an example. To conjure new love, a witch could use rose seeds, attract lovers with the flower's petals, improve love with the stem or leaves, ground love with stability by using the roots, protect or banish love with thorns, and use rose hips (fruit of roses) for marriage.

ESSENTIAL OILS

Essential oils are the liquid extracted from plants and carry the same energies as the plants from which they come. In addition to being used for magical purposes, essential oils are known for their healing properties as well. Tea tree oil, for example, fights skin infections and treats acne; cinnamon oil improves digestion; eucalyptus supports the lungs; and lavender dissolves anxiety and depression. In witchcraft, oils are often used to anoint, or rub, ourselves, our tools, and other elements of spellcraft to amplify the desired energy. As a rule, these oils should be diluted with a carrier oil such as jojoba or fractionated coconut oil before applying them to skin. That said, some may cause allergic reactions or damage certain objects.

Many witches prefer using essential oils over synthetic oils, but some essential oils are very expensive. We should never break the bank with our witchery. One possible solution is to purchase a good-smelling synthetic oil and infuse it with dried pieces from the same plant. The dried herbs will carry and spread their natural energies into the liquid.

CRYSTALS, MINERALS, AND STONES

Crystals are a highly coveted source of energy. Certain crystals, particularly quartz, can conduct energy and electricity. Not only are they beautiful, but they also hold an abundance of earth essence. Each crystal has its own unique vibration, which can be used to influence the magic we create (see the magical correlations chart on page 35). Crystals form in a variety of shapes and sizes, growing both out of the earth and deep within it. They can be purchased in their natural raw forms or as tumbled stones—a process where the mineral is polished down to a small, smooth crystal. They can also be found carved into different shapes.

 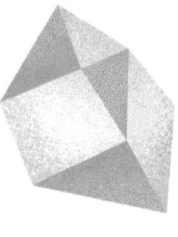

PURPOSE	HERB, RESIN, OR OIL	CRYSTAL
Attraction and Success	Catnip, rose, orange, vanilla, bay leaf, cinnamon, and High John root	Amber, citrine, green aventurine, tiger's-eye, and pyrite
Communication	Mint and blessed thistle	Amazonite, aquamarine, lapis lazuli, and turquoise
Energy	Dragon's blood, oregano, sandalwood, sunflower, and vanilla	Carnelian, citrine, garnet, and sunstone
Grounding	Coffee and pine	Bloodstone, jasper, and smoky quartz
Happiness and Peace	Chamomile, eucalyptus, neroli, lavender, and thyme	Celestite, fluorite, lepidolite, and rose quartz
Intuition and Psychic Power	Jasmine, mugwort, peppermint, star anise, and saffron	Labradorite, moonstone, and amethyst
Love and Friendship	Hibiscus, gardenia, passionflower, rose, and ylang-ylang	Emerald, rose quartz, rhodonite, and pink opal
Banishing and Protection	Basil, black pepper, onion, and garlic	Obsidian, onyx, black tourmaline, and jet
Cleansing and Purification	Copal, frankincense, lemon, sandalwood, sage, and sweetgrass	Selenite, shungite, and unakite
Wisdom	Apple, rosemary, spearmint, iris, and elderflower	Amethyst, fluorite, amazonite, sodalite, and clear quartz

COLOR

Produced by wavelengths of light, color electrifies our senses with various psychological and spiritual effects. The natural world is rich with color, and we have learned that color can have meaning, like the three colors of stoplights. Even our bodies emit color around us, called auras, which manifest differently depending on one's mental, physical, and spiritual state. Using color in magic can be done by selecting certain colored candles for a spell, different crystals, clothing, jewelry, paper, etc.

Red: passion, strength, and courage

Pink: friendship, joy, and beauty

Orange: energy, enthusiasm, and confidence

Yellow: communication, imagination, and inspiration

Green: prosperity, health, and fertility

Blue: calm, peace, and serenity

Purple: wisdom, intuition, and mysticism

Brown: stability, comfort, and foundation

Black: banishing, protection, and absorption

White: purity, spirituality, and deflection

Gray: balance, neutralization, and judgment

Silver: lunar energy, glamour, and mystery

Gold: solar energy, success, and wishes

NUMBERS

Numbers have long been considered mystical symbols. The Babylonians recorded numbers in accordance with their observation of the moon and planets, using them to better predict astrological occurrences. Egyptians considered certain numbers to be holy and supernatural. Greek philosopher and mathematician Pythagoras believed that numbers ruled the universe. In magic, the number of candles for a spell or ritual, a symbol carved into the work, the number of drops used in an oil recipe, or the number of times we recite a charm or invocation are all ways to incorporate this meaning into our magic.

1: beginnings, identity, and ego

2: partnership, balance, and emotion

3: expansion, growth, and cycles

4: stability, structure, and the physical world

5: conflict, action, and change

6: harmony, creativity, and love

7: intuition, wisdom, and introspection

8: power, justice, and career

9: completion, higher self, and success

THE TOOLS OF WITCHCRAFT

When beginning to curate our magical tool collections, we don't need to rush out and pick up every single item. In fact, the things we need might find us, if we give them the chance. By understanding what the tools are and how they are used, we can also flex and adjust with alternatives as needed.

USE WHAT'S THERE

Learning all the different ingredients and instruments needed for magic can feel overwhelming. The truth is that the only tools you will ever need as a witch are your intention and will. The purpose of specific physical witchcraft tools is to assist our magic and intensify it, but we should never feel like we have to go broke from witchcrafting.

ATHAMES AND WANDS

Both athames and wands are energy conductors that witches use to bless, empower, or enchant elements of their workings. An athame is a double-edged, magnetized blade. A wand can be made from wood, stone, or metal and usually includes a crystal at one end. While these two tools are very different, many see them as interchangeable. You can always use a letter opener (or another double-edged knife), a fallen stick that caught your eye, or the index finger of your dominant hand.

BELLS, GONGS, AND SINGING BOWLS

Bells and other musical instruments like gongs or singing bowls are fairly common tools found in witchcraft. The vibrations from the instrument help cleanse and clear a ritual space; invoke entities like deities, ancestors, and spirits; and foster a meditative state of mind.

BOOK OF SHADOWS AND GRIMOIRES

A Book of Shadows is a written documentation of a witch's practice. It includes a variety of spells, rituals, correspondence, poetry, magical thoughts, and accounts of our practice. It is a deeply personal record of our witchery. A grimoire is less personal and more of a reference source and guide to magical knowledge.

CANDLES AND INCENSE

Candles and incense are essential tools for spellcraft. Elementally, candles are a representation for fire during ritual. They come in a variety of sizes and shapes that can help in fueling our magical intent. Fire is representative of transformation. Candle magic is the art of adorning candles by anointing them with oil, rolling them in herbs, and/or carving power words or symbols into the wax.

Just like candles, incense is a powerful ingredient for rituals, representing the element of air. Incense can come in stick or cone form. It's also possible to grind our own incenses with dried herbs and resins by burning them on charcoal discs. These discs can be placed in a bowl of sand or salt inside a cauldron or fireproof dish.

CAULDRON

The cauldron is a classic staple in witch imagery. It is generally a three-legged iron pot used to burn offerings, herbs, and incense. They are relatively easy to find at occult stores and come in various sizes.

CHALICE

A chalice is a drinking vessel used specifically for rituals and spellcasting. It may be filled with a libation that is a direct ingredient of the spell or with offerings to deities, ancestors, or spirits.

MORTAR AND PESTLE

The mortar and pestle is a grinding device, usually made of metal, wood, ceramics, or hard stone, used to make magical powders and incense blends.

PENTACLE

A pentacle is a five-pointed star inside a circle and is known as the ultimate symbol of witchcraft. Each point of the star represents one of the four elements, with the fifth point representing spirit—the embodiment of us and our energy. The circle that encases the star represents the infinite possibilities of the universe and the continuum of life, death, and rebirth. A pentacle tool is traditionally a brass, silver, clay, or wooden disk that features the symbol and is used as an offering or charging plate in rituals.

DIVINATION TOOLS

Divination tools are designed to help us predict events and tap into ourselves. They assist in the development of our psychic intuition. Some common mediums for divination include oracle cards, pendulums, scrying, tarot, and tea leaf reading.

Oracle cards are a less structured alternative to tarot cards. While each deck of tarot cards contains the same cards, oracle decks are all different. Some witches will integrate an oracle card reading with a tarot card reading to gain additional clarity.

Pendulums are weights, such as a crystal point, that are hung from a fixed point on a string, cord, or chain and freely swing back and forth. When a question is asked, the movements of the pendulum are interpreted as the answers.

Scrying is the practice of gazing into an object—typically with a reflective surface—for intuitive interpretation based on the visuals or messages seen. Scrying is often done using crystal balls or a black mirror.

Tarot is a medieval occult practice that uses 78 cards to address questions about the past, present, or future. The cards are selected and combined in different spreads that contribute to the meaning of the divination, some of which will be covered in part 2. Because each card has specific meanings and energies associated with it, cards can also be used in spells and meditations to draw upon that energy.

Tea leaf reading, also known as tasseography, involves interpreting patterns and shapes of residual leaves at the bottom of a teacup after the tea has been brewed and consumed. Those seeking answers focus on a question and sip the tea, and once the cup is finished, the leaf sediments at the bottom can be interpreted.

CREATING A SELF-CARE SHRINE

Altars and shrines are deeply personal extensions of our spirituality. Depending on our practice or traditional background, altars and shrines might be considered interchangeable; however, there is a slight difference between the two. Altars are typically seen as a stage that houses our tools for ritual. A shrine, on the other hand, is a place of worship—typically devoted to a patron deity, our ancestors, angels, or other spiritual guides. Many of the solitary witches I know merge their altar and shrine into one workstation.

A self-care shrine is a dedicated magical space that honors our creative potential and spiritual essence. It's entirely up to you how you decorate your altar or shrine. The most important thing is that it makes you feel good, energized, and magical.

CASTING A CIRCLE

Circles are a sacred shape within which witches can perform spells and rituals. Within the circle, time is no longer linear. All things are happening at once in a sphere of enormous potential. The circle not only forms around us, but also above and below us, creating an egg-like shape in which to create change and magic.

Not all spells require casting a circle. I tend to reserve this practice for more ritualistic performances. There are many resources available with very detailed instructions for casting a circle, including my very own books *The Complete Book of Moon Spells* and *The GLAM Witch*. Here is a general outline for the practice:

1. Purify the space by walking in a clockwise motion with incense, a smudging stick, bell, or misting spray designed to cleanse and clear stale/negative energy.

2. Ground and center yourself to mentally prepare for the working.

3. Cast the circle by walking in a clockwise direction around your ritual space while extending an athame, wand, or the index finger of your dominant hand. Envision a stream of light pouring from your tool and forming a sphere around your space.

4. Call the elements/quarters by inviting each element into your space with their corresponding direction (earth = north, air = east, fire = south, water = west) in the same clockwise fashion.

5. If deities or ancestors are an integral part of the working, invite them into the circle.

6. Declare your intention by performing the spell or ritual.

7. Raise energy by chanting, singing, or dancing.

8. Ground yourself with food and/or a libation.

9. Release the ritual by giving thanks to the universe or your higher version of power.

10. Thank the elements at each corresponding cardinal direction, moving counterclockwise.

11. Release the circle by moving counterclockwise and declaring the ritual complete.

CONCLUSION

Our planet is rich with ingredients that can play a part in expanding our magical self-care. From the seasons to moon phases, plants to crystals, colors to numbers, and the various other tools of witchcraft, we can manifest our goals with our intentions. Now that we have learned about what goes with what and why certain ingredients are used, let's take this knowledge and put it into action.

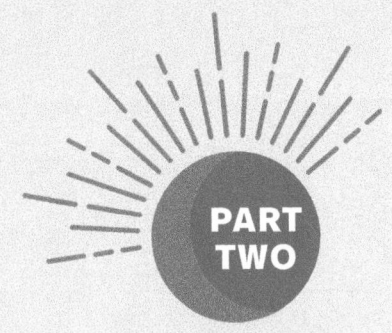

90 DAYS OF MAGICAL SELF-CARE

Welcome to part 2 of *Witchcraft for Daily Self-Care!* Having learned about witchcraft, self-care, and the ingredients of spellcasting in part 1, let us now begin a 90-day practice for summoning a new, magical you. The spells that follow are broken into six sacred categories—mind, body, spirit, environment, relationships, and personal success. The goal of these spells, rituals, and exercises is to develop a focus on magical self-care to boldly take control of our lives with the universal forces of magic.

PREPARATION AND BEST PRACTICES

Preparation is key to any successful venture. This is a great opportunity for you to learn, grow, and become more at one with yourself. It is going to take some effort, planning, and dedication—and I know you are going to rock it! Before we venture into your 90 days of magical self-care, let's go over some general best practices to make the most out of this journey.

NAVIGATING THE SPELLS

The spells, rituals, and exercises that follow are designed to be performed in order, but they don't have to be. There are many different ways to build a practice around these. For example, those who are well versed in tarot could pull a daily card first thing in the morning and allow its interpretation to determine which of these magical self-care exercises to do. Another option is bibliomancy, the divination practice of focusing the mind on what we need to work on, and randomly selecting one of the pages in part 2 for practice.

Think of these spells as a template to unleash the magic in you, and innovate at will. There is no one right way to do things, and it's important that we use our intuition for guidance. Part of magic is playing with the cards you have, so if a spell or ritual calls for an unavailable resource, simply refer to the chart on page 35 for alternatives.

TIMING

While they can be powerful, remember that spells are not a quick self-care fix. The activities here are designed with simplicity in mind. That said, feel free to add to or adjust the spellwork as necessary: Brewing a tea spell or making a batch of bath salts may take about five to 10 minutes, whereas a meditation or full-blown spell that requires a candle to fully extinguish could take an hour or longer.

WHY AREN'T MY SPELLS WORKING?

A common question, particularly among new witches is, "Why aren't my spells working?" We must exercise patience when we work magic. Time as we know it is different than universal time. We must breathe, believe, and act as if the outcome of our spells has already been received. The universe aligns with the laws of attraction. We cannot continually harp on what we have done or asked for. We must have faith in the magic we conjure and continue to go after what we want.

SELF-CARE SHOPPING LIST

Look over the spells and rituals to create a self-care shopping list that corresponds to the general or specialty ingredients needed. I've also created a list of ingredients that are commonly found in stores or online or that can be easily interchanged for others. Part of spellwork, however, is going on the hunt for the needed items and putting effort into locating them. It is always best to purchase witchy items from small businesses and independent stores. Along with the herbs, oils, crystals, and other supplies suggested in chapter 3, here is a guiding list of general supplies to have on hand:

Bowls

Candleholders

Candles

Charcoal discs

Crystals

Epsom salt

Essential oils

Heatproof bowl/cauldron

Herbs (fresh and dried)

Incense

Jojoba or fractionated coconut oil

Journal

Lighter or matches

Measuring cups/spoons

Paper

Pens/markers

Tea

MAGICAL MORNINGS

Wake up slowly each morning, fully stretching awake. In that moment, we can celebrate that there is a new day full of possibilities ahead. Go to a window and perform a pentagram salute by tracing the five-pointed star over your head and torso. Using the index finger of your dominant hand, touch the center of your forehead to your right breast, to your left shoulder, then the right shoulder, down to your left breast, and back to your forehead. Surrender to the moment and fully embrace yourself as a divine expression of magic.

EATING WITH INTENTION

Several of the 90 days of spells and rituals will incorporate magic cooking techniques. Eating is a daily occurrence, and one that we should approach with intention. Be conscious of the foods that you are consuming and how they benefit your mind, body, spirit, environment, community, and overall success.

ENGAGING ACTIVELY IN THE DAY

Whether it is simply counting steps, going for a daily walk outside, or heading to the gym—daily activity helps keep us energized. Doing so will release endorphins, which ultimately make us feel better. But beyond that, being energetic means we are making the most of our lives in the moment.

TRACKING OUR SELF-CARE FOR RESULTS

One of the best things we can do in witchcraft and self-care is track our progress. Even if we do not wish to create a formal book of shadows, journaling each day is an extremely cathartic process and can also help us do better as we go.

PRACTICING SAFE HEX

There will be no hexing here—only a reminder to witch wisely. Always make safety a priority during spellcasting. We must practice fire safety, test oils and herbs before applying them topically, and be aware of our surroundings. Some of the rituals suggest being outside; in those instances, always exercise caution and judgment. Self-care also means not putting ourselves in harm's way.

DAILY SPELLS
AND RITUALS

MIND

A Dedication to Self-Care

Let's kick off our magical self-care journey with a little self-dedication ritual. This will help further align our minds with the magic of us moving forward.

Knife	**Pen**
1 white pillar candle	**Cauldron or fireproof bowl**
Lighter or matches	**1 fresh white rose**
1 piece of paper	**Camera or smartphone**

1. Carve your name into the candle, along with any other sigils or personal symbols of power that connect to you. Lick your thumb and slide it over your carved name to seal it with your essence.

2. Light the candle and write what you pledge to achieve in the next 90 days on a piece of paper by candlelight. It can be as long or as simple as you like, but it should be personal and straight from your heart.

3. Light the paper with the flame from the candle and place it into your cauldron or fireproof bowl.

4. Say aloud: "I, (your name), dedicate myself to unlocking the magic within me. I conjure self-love, so mote it be."

5. Remove each petal from the rose and drop them into the pot of ashes while thinking about how amazing it will feel to tend to your needs.

6. Blow out the candle flame and take the pot outside. Sprinkle the mixture of ashes and petals on the earth. Take a photo of yourself to document your dedication.

7. Each day, relight your candle until it is burnt out. Save any remains from your candle in a safe place to be used in a future spell.

Fluorite Crystal Meditation

Let's dive into a relatively simple visualization meditation that can take anywhere from 10 to 30 minutes. This exercise allows us to clear our minds and tap into setting our goals with the power of fluorite.

Purple candle (optional)   **Cushion**
Lavender incense (optional)   **Fluorite crystal**
Lighter or matches

1. Create a sacred space in a place where you will not be disturbed in the morning before you start any daily responsibilities.

2. Light a purple candle to stimulate wisdom and clarity of mind and burn lavender incense for soothing energies, if you feel so inclined.

3. Sit in a comfortable position on your cushion and hold the fluorite crystal in your nondominant hand. Close your eyes and take 10 breaths, inhaling deeply through your nose and exhaling slowly through your mouth. With each breath, feel yourself drift further away from the mundane world and into a state of supreme peace. Focus your mind on your breathing and how your body feels in the moment.

4. Visualize a purple, green, and blue light softly swirling around you. As the colors envelop you, visualize them pouring into your head through your third eye. Focus on moving through your day with a clear mind, overcoming stress and daily pressures.

5. See the colors fully absorb into you. Once you feel that you are complete, take another 10 deep, slow breaths, and come back into reality. Carry the crystal with you for the day.

Happy Oil Blend

Mixing oils is one way that modern witches create potions. The power of scent can reach out and grab our attention, captivating us. Certain smells can trigger parts of the brain to recall memories, good feelings, and even states of relaxation. Today is a day to create a calming aroma to get us into a state of happiness.

1 (15-milliliter) rollerball bottle
Pinch dried lavender (optional)
Dried vanilla bean (optional)
1 mini rose quartz chip small enough to fit in the bottle (optional)
20 drops vanilla oil, for soothing energy

10 drops lavender oil, for a calming effect
5 drops bergamot oil, for joy
5 drops clary sage oil, for mood enhancement
1 drop cinnamon oil, for successful healing
Fractionated coconut oil

1. If desired, place the lavender, vanilla bean, and rose quartz chip into the rollerball bottle.

2. Into the rollerball bottle, drop the vanilla oil, lavender oil, bergamot oil, and clary sage oil, one by one. With the addition of each ingredient, focus on the specified intention of each one.

3. Add 1 drop of cinnamon oil; cinnamon is a very strong fragrance, so a little goes a lot way.

4. Add as much fractionated coconut oil as feels right. Cap the rollerball bottle and shake it vigorously.

5. Apply the oil mixture to your inner wrists, behind your ears, and your clavicle.

Blissful Sleep Spray

A good night's rest offers a chance for the mind and body to reset and recharge. It helps stimulate our mental abilities by sharpening our memories and problem-solving skills. Therefore, sound sleep is an extremely important element of self-care. For today's spell, we'll be witchcrafting a potion to help us get slumber.

1 (4-ounce) spray bottle
6 tablespoons distilled water
2 ounces unscented witch hazel
15 drops lavender oil

Tumbled amethyst crystal
(small enough to fit in
the bottle)

1. Into the spray bottle, pour the distilled water and witch hazel and mix them together in a clockwise motion. As you swirl the mixture, visualize a blissful sleep and how it will help you achieve a mental reset.

2. Add the lavender oil while saying aloud: "Essence of lavender, soothe me with your calming scent."

3. Hold the amethyst crystal in your receptive hand. Tightly make a fist around it and ask that it help guide you into a blissful state of sleep: "Amethyst, enhance my potion with your soothing frequency."

4. Gently shake your bottle and mist your pillows and sheets at bedtime with the spray as you say: "Mindful lavender and amethyst, combine your essence to help me sleep in absolute bliss."

5. Reuse the potion to mist your bed whenever you feel you need a mental magical reset.

Sound Bath Meditation

A sound bath is a meditative practice that uses sound waves to wash over you and create a feeling of peace and oneness.

1 purple candle
Lavender incense
Lighter or matches
Cushion

A bell, chime, gong,
  singing bowl, or other
  ringing instrument*
Journal
Pen

1. Create a sacred space in a place where you will not be disturbed in the morning before you start any daily responsibilities.

2. Light a purple candle to stimulate wisdom and clarity of mind, and burn lavender incense for soothing energies.

3. Sit in a comfortable position on your cushion and close your eyes. Take 10 breaths, inhaling deeply through your nose and exhaling slowly through your mouth. With each breath, feel yourself drift further away from your space and into a space between the worlds. Focus on your breathing and how your body feels in the moment.

4. Play your instrument when you feel ready, focusing on the sound. Pay attention to any sensations or thoughts that come into your mind. As they do, acknowledge them, and let them fade away organically. Continue playing the instrument, finding peace with each strike.

5. Express gratitude when you are ready to end your meditation by bowing in acknowledgment of your self-care practice. Reflect on your experience and feelings in your journal.

If you do not have a ringing instrument, you can find a variety of sound meditations on YouTube for free.

Witch Web Wisdom

We live in an age where we have all the information we could ever ask for right at our fingertips. Unfortunately, with the Internet comes a world of misinformation as well. Today's spell is about using a different kind of WWW (Witch Web Wisdom!) to find new knowledge in an area of interest.

Journal

Pen

Frankincense (diluted with a carrier oil), for a successful venture

1 apple, for wisdom

1 clear quartz crystal

Laptop computer, or smartphone

1. Write a list of things on which you would like to expand your knowledge. This could be something spiritual to help your witchery grow, an area of study, or something that could contribute to your career.

2. Anoint your wrists and neck with the frankincense oil.

3. Hold the apple in your left hand and the quartz crystal in your right hand. The left side of the body is known for absorbing and taking in energy while the right is used to direct energy.

4. Enchant your apple and crystal by stating: "Fruit of knowledge and crystal of clear vision, set me free to find the wisdom I search for easily."

5. Eat the entire apple and place the crystal on your computer.

6. Begin your quest for knowledge in the area of your choosing. As you learn, take notes on your findings to reflect back on later.

Lyrical Poetry

Words hold power. Just like a witch's spell, lyrics and poetry can create energy and further one's intent. Today's magical exercise is to create an art piece by constructing a poem from lyrics of our favorite songs. This is designed to flex the creative parts of your mind to express who you are and leave a physical representation for you to reflect on as an affirmation of your magical self.

**Computer, laptop,
   or smartphone**
**Multiple sheets of white
   lined paper**
Pen
Scissors

Bowl
Glue or tape
**1 piece of paper (color of
   your choice)**
Picture frame (optional)

1. Get settled in a quiet place that's free from distraction.

2. Using a computer, laptop, or smartphone, create a playlist of 5 to 10 of your favorite songs.

3. Write down some of your favorite lyrics in single lines on a piece of lined paper. Write down as many lyrics as you want—there is no wrong way to do this.

4. Using the scissors, cut out each lyric line as a strip of paper. Place all the strips into a bowl.

5. Close your eyes, ground yourself, then select a strip of paper from the bowl. Glue or tape the strip of paper with a song lyric to the colored sheet of paper. Do this with each strip of paper, one by one, until the bowl is empty.

6. Enchant the poem by reading or singing the lyrics aloud and placing the finished piece on your altar or shrine, or hanging it in a place that you frequent.

THE MAGICAL ART OF
ROSALEEN NORTON

Art is magic: It combines your mind, imagination, and spirit with
energy and passion in a way that affects you and others who
view or experience it. Rosaleen Norton (Australia, 1917–1979) was
one of the most prolific witch artists in history and an inspiring
role model who exemplified magical self-care. Referred to as
the Witch of Kings Cross, she caused much controversy during
the 1940s and 1950s. Her art combined occult spirituality,
supernatural themes, and sexuality—all of which were considered taboo at the time. Her rebellious work even caused police
to shut down her exhibitions and prosecute her. Regardless, she
always remained true to herself.

Enchanted Artwork

Art is a wonderful tool to enhance creative expression and mental stimulation. This magical exercise taps into the wild and free energy of your creative passion, calling upon you to mentally disconnect from the world and instead engage with your creative mind to conjure an enchanted artwork.

1 yellow candle
Lighter or matches
Music of your choice

Paint, pens, markers, crayons, or colored pencils
Canvas, board, paper, or any other blank medium

1. Set up your space so that it is comfortable and feels magical.

2. Light the yellow candle and play music to get into a joyful and artistic mindset.

3. Gather your art supplies and begin creating. Let your intuition guide you as you paint or draw. Remember that the aim to this ritual is not to be the next Michelangelo. Create whatever comes to mind using any of the methods listed below:

   • Create a power symbol or sigil that reflects a magical identity.

   • Use the words from your lyrical poem (Lyrical Poetry, page 62) as inspiration.

   • Paint or draw an herb or plant, crystal, tool, or supernatural occurrence that you find interesting.

   • Use color magic to create a monochromatic abstract piece of work based on your intention.

   • Chant a mantra, affirmation, or quote that you find inspiring.

4. Hang your finished artwork in a place you feel intuitively drawn to.

AnxieTea Bath

Tea is not just for drinking—it can also be added to your bath to create a heightened sense of relaxation and detox your body. For today's spell, we will be making an herbal tea bath to combat anxiety.

2 quarts water

Saucepan

⅓ cup dried, culinary-grade chamomile, for stress relief*

⅓ cup dried, culinary-grade mint, for uplifting energy*

⅓ cup dried, culinary-grade valerian root, for harmony*

2 tablespoons Epsom salt

White candles

Lighter or matches

1. Bring 2 quarts of water to a boil in a saucepan. Remove from the heat once it reaches the boiling point.

2. Add the chamomile, mint, and valerian root to the saucepan. Stir in a clockwise motion and enchant your herbs by saying the following: "Chamomile, mint, and valerian root, herbs of relaxing energy, soothe my mind to reduce anxiety."

3. Remove the saucepan from the heat, cover it, and let it steep.

4. Draw a warm bath while the tea steeps. Add the Epsom salt to the bathwater for relaxation and soothing the skin and muscles.

5. Light some white candles and dim the lights.

6. Pour yourself a cup of tea and set it on the ledge of your bathtub. Strain the remaining tea into the bath.

7. Enter the bath and bask in the calming water. As you feel your body relaxing, drink your tea and visualize your body glowing with a radiant and restorative white light.

*Consult with a primary care physician before drinking any teas to ensure that there are no adverse side effects or interactions with any prescriptions you may be taking or conditions you may have.

Freeze Comparison

Being envious of others' talents, successes, and situations is not only unproductive and damaging to our self-care, but it can also stunt our personal growth. All the energy that could be put into a feeling of envy can instead be productively channeled into growing stronger and successful in our own ways. This spell is designed to freeze those feelings of envy and self-doubt and free our minds to be more fruitful.

Piece of paper

Black pen

Scissors

Garlic cloves (1 for each situation or person)

Tape

Freezable container

Water

1. Think about all the situations or people you are envious of and write their names on the paper with a black pen. Cut each of these names out of the paper with a pair of scissors.

2. Wrap each piece of paper around a garlic clove, which is known for naturally exorcising negativity, and secure the bundles with tape.

3. Visualize yourself letting go of these emotions and spending your time working toward your own goals.

4. Speak from the heart as you bind the garlic and say: "I bind these comparative thoughts in me and release my envy. Without this jealousy may I move forward more productively."

5. Place the paper and garlic bundles in a freezable container and fill it with water.

6. Place the container in the back of your freezer, where it can remain undisturbed.

7. Observe how much your feelings of envy have lessened in a month and remove the container from the freezer.

8. Bury the remains outdoors in a place you do not frequently cross.

Ace of Swords Tarot Spread

Today, we will use tarot, the ancient art of divination, to determine how to better nourish our mental health. We'll be using the Ace of Swords, the strongest representation of mental clarity, new ideas, communication, and our inner thoughts.

Deck of tarot cards   **Pen**
Journal

1. Remove the Ace of Swords from your tarot deck and place it faceup in front of you.

2. Shuffle the deck and as you do, drift out of your current state of mind and ask the universe, ancestors, god/dess, or your version of a higher power what it is that you need to know to improve your mental health.

3. Cut the deck into three piles in a horizontal line under the Ace of Swords. Turn the top card of each pile over and interpret the reading using the symbolism of the card and your understanding of it:

   Card 1: Unresolved Past: The first card shows what to let go of. This situation is causing a blockage or strain on your current state of mind.

   Card 2: Current State of Mind: This is a representation of your present mental state and how it has been impacted by your past circumstances.

   Card 3: Recommend Path: This card represents the advice for how you should move forward.

4. Reflect upon your spread and record your findings in a journal. Create an action plan for achieving the recommendations from the spread.

Candle Spell to Surrender Fear

Today, we will perform candle magic to release fear that may be holding us back to move forward with a freer mind, feel lighter, and find more joy.

Knife	**Plate**
1 black chime candle,	**Dried basil**
for banishing*	**Candleholder**
3 drops black pepper oil	**Lighter or matches**

1. Using a knife, carve your name into one side of the black chime candle. On the other side, carve a fear—using words or a symbol—that is holding you back.

2. Turn the candle upside down and carefully chip away at the base with your carving tool so the wick is exposed. As you do, visualize yourself chipping away at the fear itself.

3. Lick your thumb and slide it over your carved name to seal it with your essence. Place three drops of the black pepper oil on the carving.

4. Place the candle on a plate and sprinkle the basil onto the candle, massaging it into the creases while continuing to visualize your fear.

5. Place the candle into a holder upside down, so that your freshly carved base is the tip. Light the exposed wick as you proclaim: "I surrender my fear. I surrender (<u>state your fear</u>)."

6. Gaze into the flame and reflect honestly upon this fear and how it has held you back and how surrendering it will improve your life.

7. Allow the candle to burn completely out. After it has cooled, place any remains in the trash immediately so that it is no longer in your space.

*Chime candles have a burn time of 2 to 2½ hours. Please allow yourself enough time to let this candle burn completely out, safely, and under supervision.

Release Sadness

Let's go deep and use the power of common culinary staples to release any feelings of sadness that might be standing in the way of our self-care progress.

Small square piece of paper
Pen
1 garlic clove (or 1 teaspoon garlic powder)
1 rosemary sprig (or 1 teaspoon dried)

1 yellow onion
Cutting board
Kitchen knife
Large bowl
Shovel

1. Write down your name and any lingering feelings that make you sad on a piece of paper. These could be past traumas or failures.

2. Crush the garlic clove and remove the rosemary leaves from the sprig. Add them to the bowl.

3. Continue to focus on what makes you sad while you execute the remainder of the spell.

4. Place the onion on its side on a cutting board. Use your knife to cut off the root and top end of the onion. Peel off the outer skin. While doing so, visualize your external emotional wall being pulled back. Place the skin in the bowl.

5. Cut the onion through the center and place the piece of paper with your name and feelings inside. Position the onion back together, as if it were whole again, and dice the onion. As you do, welcome any tears that may come. Say: "Onion, bulb that was buried deep, release my sadness with these tears that I weep."

6. Add the chopped onion and paper to the bowl.

7. Take the bowl and its contents outside, setting it aside to dig a shallow hole with the shovel in the earth. Drop the mixture into the ground and cover it, relinquishing your sadness to the earth.

Movie Magic Marathon

For a lot of people, self-care means a day of lounging on the couch or in bed and binge-watching TV. So that is exactly what you are going to do, focusing on witchy entertainment for the day! This will feel restorative after the past two days of emotionally intense spells.

Your favorite incense
Lighter or matches
Yellow candle, for inspiration
Neroli oil, for joy and relaxation
Witch movies or TV shows
  (see page 71 for suggestions)

TV, laptop, computer, or iPad
Journal or pad of paper
Pen
Your favorite snacks and
  beverages (optional)

1. Create a magical nest of pillows, blankets, snacks, and anything else that comforts you.

2. Light the incense stick and move it around your space in a clockwise direction to harmonize the energies in your nest. As you do this, concentrate on how relaxed and joyous you will ultimately feel after your mental health day.

3. Anoint your yellow candle with the neroli oil. Light the candle with a match and say: "Magical movies for me to see, to help unlock the magic within me, may I escape with fantasy, and relax here joyously."

4. Set the candle in the center of your space (if you can do so safely) so that it is positioned between you and the screen on which you'll be watching movies.

5. Select the films you'd like to watch and begin your marathon. While you do, jot down any ideas or inspirations that come to you. These can be quotes, recipes, or other areas you may wish to explore in the world of witchcraft.

SILVER SCREEN WITCHERY

Movies and television can offer a mental rest while also stimulating creativity and excitement. Here are some of my favorite witchy movies and television shows to watch and feel inspired to do magic!

Movies

→ *Bell, Book and Candle* (1958)

→ *The Craft* (1996)

→ *Death Becomes Her* (1992)

→ *Gretel & Hansel* (2020)

→ *Harry Potter franchise* (2001–2011)

→ *Hocus Pocus* (1993)

→ *The Love Witch* (2016)

→ *Practical Magic* (1998)

→ *Simply Irresistible* (1999)

→ *Stardust* (2007)

→ *The Witches* (1990 & 2020)

→ *Woman on Top* (2000)

Television

→ *American Horror Story: Apocalypse* (2018)

→ *American Horror Story: Coven* (2013)

→ *Bewitched* (1964–1972)

→ *Brujos* (2017–2018)

→ *Buffy the Vampire Slayer* (1997–2003)

→ *Charmed* (1998–2006 & 2018–)

→ *The Chilling Adventures of Sabrina* (2018–2020)

→ *The Good Witch* (2015–)

→ *Juju* (2019–)

→ *Mad Mad House* (2004)

→ *Motherland: Fort Salem* (2020–)

→ *Salem* (2014–2017)

→ *True Blood* (2008–2014)

→ *The Vampire Diaries* (2009–2017)

→ *Witches of East End* (2013–2014)

Blooming Self-Love Spell

An essential part of self-care is loving ourselves. The best way to do so is to really believe that we are worthy of love. Today, we will work a spell to boost our sense of self-love and encourage self-appreciation.

Pink blooming flower
Planting pot and soil
Rose incense stick
Lighter or matches

Lock of hair or nail clippings
Rose quartz crystal
Water

1. Before conducting the spell, purchase a flower that blooms with pink flowers, such as an orchid or rose.

2. Select any pot or other decorative elements that you think are appropriate and set them up in your preferred spot. It should be a place that you see and interact with daily while also being an ideal location for your plant to thrive.

3. Light your rose incense stick and trace a pentagram over the plant with the smoke to clear it of any stagnant energy.

4. Holding the plant, say: "As my self-love blossoms help me see, that all the love I need is inside me."

5. Dig a hole in the potting soil and place in it unique pieces of you, such as a lock of hair or nail clippings, and the rose quartz. Cover them with the soil.

6. Pour water over the freshly covered hole and feel the soothing and emotional element of water saturate you.

7. Visit the plant each morning, caring for the plant as it grows, and visualize your self-love growing with it.

BODY

Love Your Body

A powerful aspect of self-care is the love and appreciation we give to ourselves. Nothing screams self-care more than unapologetically loving the skin we are in. This next spell is designed to open the door for body positivity.

Knife

1 pink chime candle

Rose oil

Pinch orange zest

Lighter or matches

1 fresh pink or orange rose

Full-length mirror

Bowl

1. Use a knife to carve your name into the pink chime candle.

2. Anoint the candle with 6 drops of rose oil and rub it down with a pinch of orange zest.

3. Light the candle and hold it in your right hand. Hold a pink or orange rose in your left hand. Standing in front of the mirror, gaze into the reflection of your eyes and say: "By flame and flower, I acknowledge my beauty and shower my body with positivity."

4. Set down the candle and pull the petals off the rose, tossing them above your head to shower yourself with its beauty.

5. Gather your rose petals from the floor and place them in a bowl on your altar or shrine along with the candle. Allow the candle to safely burn out.

6. Take the petals outside about a week later, after they have dried, and toss them into the wind, symbolically sharing your beauty with the world.

Purification Bath Salts

Epsom salt baths are a great way to physically detox your body. Magically, salt is used to absorb negative energies and is a powerful purifying substance. Today, we'll make a ritual bath salt blend to promote relaxation of the body and purify our physical temples.

Mixing bowl
7 ounces Epsom salt
Handful dried rose
  petals or buds
1 teaspoon lemon or orange zest
Pinch dried rosemary
2 drops tea tree oil

2 drops lemon oil
2 drops rose oil
2 drops rosemary oil
1 (8-ounce) storage container
Strip of white paper
Pen

1. In a mixing bowl, combine the salts, rose petals or buds, lemon or orange zest, and rosemary.

2. Add 2 drops each of the tea tree, lemon, rose, and rosemary oils. Stir the blend in a counterclockwise circle to represent the banishing of energy.

3. Transfer your salts to a storage container.

4. Write "PURIFICATION" on a piece of paper and kiss it three times. Place the paper into the container and place the container on your altar or shrine for the day.

5. Draw a warm bath in the evening. Add a couple handfuls of the salt into the water and immerse yourself in the bath for 20 minutes. As you do, visualize all the negative energy being pulled out of you and into the water.

6. Rinse and dry yourself off. Use your remaining salts again whenever you want to feel relaxed.

A Sacred Walk

Walking in nature is one of the best ways to clear the mind and energize the body. Today's spell is designed to help us embrace our magical journeys by walking without any agenda or expectation—allowing ourselves to be led wherever we need to be. Allow yourself at least 30 minutes.

Quartz crystal   **Journal**

Comfortable shoes   **Pen**

Smartphone or camera

1. Program your quartz crystal to guide you on your adventure by placing the crystal on the ground between your feet and asking it to bless your walk and lead you however it may. Visualize a white light extending from the crystal and into your feet.

2. Pick up the crystal when you feel ready and place it in your pocket.

3. Put on comfortable walking shoes and go outside—heading nowhere in particular. Allow your feet and intuition to guide you. You may either listen to songs that inspire you or listen to the nature flowing around you.

4. Pay attention to your surroundings and align your state of being with the natural world around you. Take photos of the scenery. Look back on those images in the evening before bed and journal about anything that comes to you.

Eucalyptus Shower Spell

Eucalyptus is a staple in spa treatments. Inhaling vaporous steam and eucalyptus clears the respiratory system and is especially beneficial for those who suffer from asthma and sinusitis. This magical shower spell can turn a bathroom into a luxurious and invigorating steam room.

1 bunch eucalyptus
Twine
Orange candle, for energy
  and confidence

Eucalyptus oil (optional)
Lighter or matches

1. Gather a bundle of fresh eucalyptus. Clip the ends so that the bunch is even in length.

2. Secure the bundle with the twine and speak to it, letting it know what you want it to do for you. You may wish to say something like: "Eucalyptus, with your healing scent, help me breathe in."

3. Hang the bundle from your showerhead and run the hot water.

4. Light the orange candle. (You may wish to anoint it first with eucalyptus oil for extra oomph.) Orange candles are great for bodywork because the color represents vitality, energy, and confidence associated with a healthy body.

5. Step into your shower and enjoy your magical sauna. Take deep breaths of the steamy, therapeutic mist while visualizing its healing powers being absorbed into your body.

6. Use your bundle for a maximum of 7 days. When you're ready to discard it, place the bundle in a location outside where it can remain undisturbed, and offer your gratitude for the plant's healing powers.

Sensual Skin Potion

Moisturizing reduces the potential for skin problems such as dryness, oily skin, and acne. Today's exercise involves crafting a witchy moisturizing blend to leave your skin feeling sensually supple and radiant with beauty.

Mixing bowl
1 cup unscented lotion
¼ teaspoon silver or gold mica
3 drops rose oil, for beauty
3 drops lavender oil,
   for serenity

3 drops vanilla oil, for
   sensual energy
3 drops frankincense oil,
   for purification
3 pieces tumbled rose quartz
Whisk
1 (8-ounce) bottle or container

1. In a mixing bowl, combine the unscented lotion and silver or gold mica.

2. Add 3 drops each of the rose, lavender, vanilla, and frankincense oils to the bowl, calling upon their unique energies to assist in your concoction. Say: "Rose, help my beauty to shine. Lavender, may my skin be smooth and alive. Vanilla, maximize my sensuality. Frankincense, purify my body."

3. Hold the tumbled rose quartz in your left hand. Say: "Smooth crystals of beauty, ignite my skin with sensuality."

4. Add the crystals to the bowl and whisk your potion in a clockwise motion.

5. Transfer the mixture to the 8-ounce bottle. Apply the mixture to your body and shine like the god/dess you are!

Elderberry Syrup

Elderberry is a powerful herb used in magic for protection and defense as well as boosting the immune system. This recipe has been perfected by my beloved friends E. V. Heart and Jenni Love. Before consuming elderberry syrup, be sure to determine if there are any counterindications with supplements or medications you're taking.

Saucepan

4 cups filtered water

⅔ cup dried black elderberries or 1⅓ cups fresh or frozen elderberries

2 tablespoons fresh or dried gingerroot

1 tablespoon dried echinacea

1 tablespoon dried rose hips

1 tablespoon dried orange peel

2 teaspoons dried elder flowers

1 teaspoon ground cinnamon or 1 cinnamon stick

½ teaspoon whole cloves or ground cloves

Spoon or flat utensil

Strainer

Glass jar or bowl

1 cup raw honey

Glass bottle

1. Into a medium saucepan, pour the water, elderberries, gingerroot, echinacea, rose hips, orange peel, elder flowers, cinnamon, and cloves.

2. Bring the mixture to a boil, then cover the saucepan and reduce the heat to a simmer for 45 minutes to an hour, or until the liquid has reduced by half.

3. Remove the mixture from the heat and let it cool enough to be handled.

4. Using a spoon or flat utensil, carefully mash the berries in the saucepan.

5. Pour the mixture through a strainer into a glass jar or bowl. Discard the elderberries and let the liquid cool to lukewarm.

6. Add the honey, stirring well to combine, when the brew is no longer hot.

7. Pour the syrup into a glass bottle for storage. Keep refrigerated. The syrup will have a shelf life of 2 to 3 months.

THE HEALTHY WITCH

What does it mean to be healthy? "Healthy" is not a one- size-fits-all state of being. Each of our body types requires different compositions for optimal wellness. Being healthy is ensuring that you are receiving the proper nutrients for sustainability and eating in a way that energizes your body. Eat the things that fuel your body, drink to hydrate yourself, move to stay energized and connect to your environment, and rest to restore your vitality. And, to quote my friend and fellow witch Fiona Horne, "Don't even drink shit coffee!"

Favorite Feast

Cooking magic is a fun and powerful way to fuel our bodies while fueling our intentions. Today, we'll make a favorite meal from scratch, infusing it with desire to further intensify our magical goals.

Organic locally grown ingredients, for your favorite meal

White candle

Lighter or matches

1. Research the characteristics associated with the various ingredients needed to make your dish. You can do so by cross-referencing the chart on page 35 or consulting online resources, such as TheMagickalCat.com, or Googling "metaphysical properties of (ingredient name)."

2. Take note of any details that might better explain why you enjoy the meal. Do the ingredients further intensify your current goals? If you find that an ingredient's energy does not match with your overall intentions, see what ingredient you can substitute for it that has a more congruent energy.

3. Light the white candle while you cook your meal to reflect the harmonious energies you are stirring up with your cooking magic.

4. Visualize the first time you ever had this dish while you make it and how delicious it tasted.

5. Bless the food before eating it by saying: "With each bite may I savor the joy that comes from your flavor."

6. Eat your meal by candlelight. As you enjoy your feast, visualize your body being filled with the love that went into creating it.

Detoxifying Body Brew

Water helps our bodies deliver enough nutrients to all our cells, regulate body temperature, and elevate mood. The water content in watermelons is a delicious way to get hydrated. Magically, the fruit is associated with healing and peace. This detoxifying potion helps banish energetic blockages in the body while ensuring that we're well hydrated.

Pitcher

6 cups cubed seedless watermelon

1 cucumber, cut into slices

6 fresh mint leaves

6 fresh basil leaves

1 lime

1 cup water

4 rose quartz crystals (optional)

Blender

Pinch salt

Chalice or cup

1. In a pitcher, place the watermelon, cucumber, mint, and basil.

2. Cut the lime in half and squeeze the juice into the pitcher.

3. Pour the cup of water into the pitcher, then place it in your refrigerator for 6 hours to chill and soften the fruit.

4. Place 4 pieces of rose quartz around the base of the pitcher in the refrigerator to stimulate soothing energies, if you so wish.

5. After 6 hours, pour the contents of the pitcher into a blender. Before turning it on, add a pinch of salt and enchant your potion with these words: "Cleansing crystal from the sea, blend with this potion to hydrate me."

6. Flip the switch and blend your brew.

7. Pour the contents into your chalice or another cup. As you drink your watermelon body brew, visualize it flowing through your body and detoxifying your system.

Signature Scent Body Spray

A signature scent is a wonderful way to enchant a room with your persona. The body spray we'll be *witch*-crafting today is designed to represent your essence by combining the top, mid, and base notes of perfumery with the extra oomph of glamour magic.

Tumbled quartz crystal (small enough to fit in the bottle)
1 (30-milliliter) spray bottle
5 milliliters unscented witch hazel

30 drops essential oil*
15 milliliters distilled water
Funnel

* See chart in step 1.

1. Use the chart below to determine which essential oils you will use. Refer back to page 35 to check the magical properties of the oils if needed. I personally love a blend of black pepper, rose, and musk.

NOTE	RATIO	PURPOSE	CATEGORY	SCENTS
Top	20 percent 6 drops	The first impression	Citrus/spice	Bergamot, black pepper, clary sage, lavender, lemon, orange
Mid	50 percent 15 drops	The main, dominant scent profile	Floral/spice	Cinnamon, ginger, jasmine, neroli, rose, ylang-ylang
Base	30 percent 9 drops	Lingers on the skin the longest	Exotic/woodsy	Cedar, frankincense, musk, patchouli, sandalwood, vanilla

CONTINUED >

2. Place the crystal in the bottle and add the witch hazel. Add your essential oils: top, mid, then base notes. Pour in the distilled water. Cap the mixture and swirl in a clockwise motion saying: "Crystal from the earth and fragrance of me, enchant my presence so that others may see the potent and powerful beauty of me!"

3. Spritz your body with your signature scent and carry on with your day.

SEX MAGIC

Witches have healthy views on sexuality, seeing all acts of love and pleasure as divine expressions of life. This is due to the connection between the fertility and abundance of the land and our physical bodies. Witchcraft also blends the pleasure of orgasm with spiritual reverence. Sexual energy and pleasure can be harnessed to manifest our goals and desires. This form of magic can be practiced with partners but is most commonly done through masturbation, though the expression of sexual energy is creative and can be released in nonphysical ways as well. We should never feel pressured to do anything that makes us feel uncomfortable. Those who are not sexually active can still use sex magic by preserving sexual energy and transmuting it into creative potential.

Beauty Mask

This spell combines powerful and healing ingredients known to promote glowing, radiant skin. One application of this beauty mask will leave you looking like the glamorous god/dess you are!

**1 organic egg, for vitality
and youth**

Mixing bowl

**4 drops tea tree essential oil,
for harmony**

**1 tablespoon honey,
for attraction**

**1 tablespoon freshly squeezed
lemon juice, for cleansing**

Whisk

Applicator brush or cotton ball

1. Pre-rinse and dry your face.

2. Crack the egg on the side of the mixing bowl into two halves. Transfer the yolk between the shells so that the egg white drips into the bowl. Egg whites act as an astringent for the skin.

3. Set aside the yolk.

4. Add the 4 drops of tea tree oil to the bowl. Tea tree oil fights acne, in addition to having many antiseptic qualities.

5. Add the honey (an antibacterial agent that assists in reducing scars and inflammation) to the bowl.

6. Squeeze 1 tablespoon of lemon juice into the bowl to reduce skin discoloration and blotchiness.

7. While you whisk the contents of the bowl in a counterclockwise motion and visualize a perfect complexion, chant the following six times: "Radiant and divine will be the complexion of mine!"

8. Use an applicator brush or cotton ball to brush the mixture onto your entire face, avoiding contact with the eyes or lips.

9. Let the concoction dry on your face completely, 15 to 20 minutes.

10. Rinse your face with warm water and gently pat it dry.

A Glamour Spell

When using intent to fuel our external personas, we create glamour magic. This spell is designed to enchant our clothing for the day and help us feel that much more magical and glamorous.

Outfit of choice
Rose incense

Lighter or matches
Mirror (ideally full-length)

1. Select an outfit that makes you feel confident and attractive as you get ready to face the day. You can also use your intent and color magic (page 36) to amplify your goals for the day.

2. Light your incense and trace smoke pentagrams over your clothing on a hanger. If needed, push the smoke with your breath onto the fabric. As you do this, say: "Glamour, glamour—come to me! May my splendor be seen by everybody!"

3. Dress yourself and stand in front of a mirror with your arms out in front of you. Place your palms directly on the mirror. Look deep into your eyes and say this spell: "By the power of me, may others see, the version of myself I wish to be."

4. Close your eyes and visualize a glowing stream of light pouring from your right hand into your reflection and back into you through your left hand, creating a circle of energy between you and your reflection. In this moment, you are merging with your reflection.

5. Continue to visualize yourself in a sparkling, glowing light as you go about your day, using the energy of attraction to manifest your goals.

Ecstatic Dance

Many different magical systems incorporate dance in rituals as a way to raise energy and honor deities, ancestors, and spirits. Through dance, we can direct our physical movement and manipulate it as an additional energy source to fuel our intentions. Today, you will set aside some time for an ecstatic dance ritual—a trance-like dance state where you move freely to the music of your choice.

A selection of your favorite songs

Computer, laptop, or smartphone
Comfortable, loose clothing

1. Create a playlist of at least 5 to 10 songs on your computer, laptop, or smartphone, choosing songs that make you want to dance.

2. Play the music on an available device—your phone, laptop, speaker system, television, etc.

3. Begin moving by fully stretching your body to increase flexibility and range of motion.

4. Allow yourself to be guided by the rhythm of the music once you're well stretched, moving your body to the sound.

5. Focus on the current tasks and situations in your life on this day. How do you want them to unfold? Visualize your desires manifesting. Use your body as an instrument to manifest magic by raising its energy in service of your intentions through movement.

6. Continue to move and dance intuitively for as long as you see fit.

7. Ground your energy by sitting, resting, and breathing calmly to lower your heart rate once you feel you're done.

Stress Relief Self-Massage

Massage eases stress, anxiety, and physical tension. This next exercise is a magically charged solo massage for stress relief. Slowing down and rounding out our movements creates fluid motion that stimulates relaxation.

Sandalwood incense

Lighter or matches

1 (2-ounce) bottle carrier oil, like sweet almond or jojoba oil

4 drops ylang-ylang oil

4 drops bergamot oil

4 drops geranium oil

1. Light your incense.

2. Mix your massage oil by adding the drops of each essential oil into the 2-ounce bottle of carrier oil. Cap it and shake the mixture well.

3. Sit in a comfortable position. Breathe in and out deeply.

4. Kiss your hands. Tell them you love them. Tell them how much you love and appreciate what they do for you.

5. Touch both hands to the top of your head as if you were holding an egg on top of it. Apply pressure and slowly extend your fingers outward until your palms are resting on your head. Retract back to the "egg position," creating a squeezing motion. Move your head around however feels best to you.

6. Apply a dime-size amount of oil onto your hands and rub it in.

7. Bring both hands to where the back of your head meets your neck. Position your hands on both sides of the spine (not directly on the spine). Gently apply pressure and spread your fingertips out.

8. Gently massage your clavicle region, shoulders, upper back, and arms, firmly rounding off your movements in a continuous motion. Use more oil if you need to.

9. Remember to move slowly; you are not in a rush.

My Body, My Temple

Today, we will explore the raw, primal energy of personal pleasure. There are several different ways this ritual can be accomplished, depending on your personal preferences: as solo sex magic or as a mindful meditation on the body, honoring it as the sacred temple it is.

1 red candle
Dragon's blood incense
Lighter or matches
Patchouli oil diluted with jojoba
   or fractionated coconut oil

Paper
Pen

1. Choose a comfortable and safe space where you can relax and be undisturbed.

2. Light your candle and incense. Dim the lights and take in the energy of the sensual atmosphere you have created.

3. Anoint yourself with the patchouli oil on your clavicle and pulse points.

4. Caress your body gently, however feels right for you, allowing yourself to embrace the soothing pleasure of your own touch.

5. Chant the following incantation over and over for as long as feels right to you: "My body is my temple. My touch is my pleasure. I am sacred and powerful."

6. Focus on how miraculous your body is and all that it does to energize and protect you, while remaining sensuous and beautiful.

7. Use the paper and pen to write a list of ways that you will continue to treat your body like the magnificent and sensual temple that it is.

8. Place your list on your altar or shrine following your ritual to serve as a reminder of how sacred you are.

Treat Yourself Cookies

For the last day of body spells, we will treat ourselves with cardamom (known for amplifying joy) white chocolate chip cookies. This recipe comes from Christina Harris, the ultimate queen of baking. The recipe makes about 20 cookies and takes 45 minutes to prepare.

Large bowl
1 cup softened unsalted butter
¾ cup granulated sugar
¾ cup light brown sugar
2 eggs (room temperature)
1 teaspoon almond extract
½ teaspoon vanilla extract
Medium bowl
3 cups flour

2 teaspoons ground cardamom
1 teaspoon baking soda
1 teaspoon salt
1½ cups white chocolate chips
1 to 3 cookie sheets
Silicone baking mat or
** parchment paper**
Cooling rack

1. Preheat the oven to 350ºF.

2. In a large bowl, mix the softened butter, granulated and brown sugars, and eggs until completely combined.

3. Add the almond extract and vanilla and stir to combine.

4. In the medium bowl, combine the flour, cardamom, baking soda, and salt.

5. Gradually add the dry mixture to the wet mixture until it is well combined.

6. Stir in the white chocolate chips.

7. Cover a cookie sheet with a silicone baking mat or parchment paper. Roll the cookie dough into balls slightly smaller than the size of a golf ball, and place 8 balls on each standard cookie sheet.

8. Bake for 9 to 12 minutes, rotating the tray halfway through. Cookies should be slightly underbaked.

9. Cool on the tray for 5 minutes, then transfer to a cooling rack.

10. Repeat steps 7 to 9 if you have any remaining dough.

11. Enjoy your cookies. As you do, savor each bite.

SPIRIT

Chakra Meditation

Today, we'll transition into taking care of the spirit with a chakra meditation. Chakras are vortexes of energy in our bodies that contribute to our energetic vitality, harmonizing the mind, body, and spirit.

Rainbow or white candle   **Yoga mat, sarong, or cushion**
Lighter or matches

1. Light your rainbow or white candle and place it at the top of your yoga mat. (If you don't have a yoga mat on hand, you can use a sarong or comfortable cushion.)

2. Lie on the mat so that the candle is just above your head. Rest your hands so they are palms up. Get comfortable and stretch out.

3. Close your eyes and take 7 deep breaths (one for each chakra), inhaling deeply through your nose and exhaling slowly through your mouth. With each breath, feel yourself drift further into a meditative state.

4. Using the chart on page 97, visualize a pulsating wheel of color spinning at each chakra point, starting at the root. When you feel as though you have fully connected to one chakra, move to the next.

5. Visualize a stream of white light connecting each of the chakras once you've activated your crown chakra. Moving backward, slowly visualize the pulsating wheel of color at your root close-up, moving all the way up to your crown.

CHAKRA	COLOR	POSITION	HOME OF	FOCUS
Root	Red	Tailbone	Foundation	Find security
Sacral	Orange	Below the navel	Creativity and sexuality	Embrace personal passions
Solar plexus	Yellow	Top of abdomen	Self-esteem and will	Reclaim personal power and control
Heart	Green	Center of chest	Love	Express love to yourself and others
Throat	Blue	Center of neck	Communication	Communicate your needs effectively
Third eye	Indigo	Between the eyes	Intuition	See beyond what is in front of you
Crown	Violet	Top of head	Higher self	Obtain enlighten-ment

Astrological Self-Care

We are all made of the same materials of which stars are made. Today's spell uses our zodiac signs for astrology-based self-care.

Knife

Candle in the color of the element corresponding to your zodiac sign (earth = green, air = yellow, fire = red, and water = blue)

Lighter or matches

Computer, laptop, or smartphone, or a book relevant to your zodiac sign

1. Using a knife, carve the symbol of your zodiac sign into the candle. (Consult the chart on page 99.)

2. Light the candle and do some reading on your sign by candlelight using any relevant book or the web.

3. Use the chart on page 99 to complete the listed activity in whichever way you are intuitively inspired to do.

4. Compare the activity to the research of your sign you conducted earlier and reflect on how meaningful the activity is to your sign's self-care.

SIGN	SYMBOL	ELEMENT	DATES	ACTIVITY
Aries		Fire	March 21–April 19	Be physically active
Taurus		Earth	April 20–May 20	Buy yourself flowers or chocolates
Gemini		Air	May 21–June 21	Write something creative
Cancer		Water	June 22–July 22	Spend time with family
Leo		Fire	July 23–August 22	Indulge in pampering yourself
Virgo		Earth	August 23–September 22	Reorganize your home
Libra		Air	September 23–October 23	Have a magical makeover
Scorpio		Water	October 24–November 21	Explore your sensuality
Sagittarius		Fire	November 22–December 21	Read a philosophical or spiritual book
Capricorn		Earth	December 22–January 19	Build your career
Aquarius		Air	January 20–February 18	Do something social
Pisces		Water	February 19–March 20	Create an art project

Facing the Shadow

To fully benefit from our divinity, we must first confront our shadow selves. While this next meditation has the potential to bring up messy emotions, it is a liberating experience that can help us reach a higher state of being. The meditation should take anywhere from 30 to 60 minutes.

Binaural beats meditation music (I recommend "Shadow Work Meditation 0.25 Hz Binaural Beats" by Sonic Elevator on YouTube)

Knife
Black chime candle
Lighter or matches
Journal
Pen

1. Wait until nighttime to perform this ritual in total darkness.

2. Prepare a space where you will be undisturbed.

3. Play your binaural beats as you settle into a relaxing position.

4. Carve your first name backward into one side of the candle. Carve your last name backward into the other side of the candle. Lick your thumb and trace it over your carvings, sealing the candle with your physical essence.

5. Light the black candle.

6. Lick your thumb and index finger, and extinguish the candle by pinching your wet fingers around the flame. State: "I extinguish this light so that I can meet my darkness."

7. Reflect on your shadow. Ask yourself to think about difficult emotions such as shame, anger, unresolved hurt, and secret desires. Ask yourself what triggers you emotionally. The purpose of this is to feel more equipped to handle these emotions when they surface.

8. Record any ideas, thoughts, or visions you had in your journal for deeper reflection once you've finished your meditation.

Sacri-Vice

Sacrifice is an important spiritual tool. To obtain, we must be willing to let go. Sacrifice is generally seen as an offering made particularly to a deity or spiritual guide. Today, we will be making personal sacrifices to affirm our commitments to self-care.

Small black candle   **Mirror**
Lighter or matches

1. Grab a small, black candle upon waking and head to your bathroom.

2. Light your candle while standing in front of your bathroom mirror.

3. Look into the reflection of your eyes and focus on something you wish to sacrifice for one day. Perhaps this is a vice like smoking or drinking, or you might even give up using your voice for the day. The choice is yours; however, it needs to be something that will be missed.

4. Blow out the candle, sealing your promise of your sacrifice to the universe.

5. Return to the mirror with the candle at bedtime. Light it, and as you do, think about how your sacrifice has felt.

6. Give your thanks for the strength to carry through with your sacrifice as you blow out the candle.

Divine Yourself

Each of us is a representation of spirit—an expression of divine consciousness. Today's ritual is designed to honor and celebrate our own inner gods and goddesses.

Figurine or photo that exemplifies your inner divinity

White, silver, or gold candle

Nag champa incense

Lighter or matches

Bowl

4 tablespoons white cosmetic clay

4 teaspoons white tea, cooled

2 teaspoons aloe vera gel

2 drops rose oil

2 drops sandalwood oil

Charcuterie or fruit plate

Wine, champagne, or nonalcoholic celebratory beverage of choice (optional)

White sheet, wrap, robe, or lingerie

1. In the evening, select a space that is large enough to stretch out and move around in.

2. Place pillows and blankets on the floor to make it more comfortable. Create a small shrine that includes the figurine, white candle, incense, and other ingredients.

3. Wrap yourself in a white sheet similar to a toga or put on any other item of comfortable and luxurious clothing, or choose to be naked or *skyclad*.

4. Light your candle and incense. In the bowl, mix the clay and tea. Add the aloe vera and essential oils. Stir the ingredients in a clockwise direction to create a smooth paste.

5. Anoint your exposed skin with the clay concoction, closing your eyes as you do and honoring the god/dess within. Let the clay dry on your skin.

6. Stand in the center of your space and declare yourself an expression of god/dess with these words: "May the divinity in me come forth—merge with me in this time of honor. You are within and all around me. As I worship you, I honor me—my divinity."

7. Spend the remainder of the evening partying like the god/dess you are—snacking on delicious foods, listening to music, dancing in your space, reading your favorite book, or creating works of art.

8. The ritual is complete; wash the clay off of your skin and apply moisturizer.

LILITH: THE GODDESS OF SELF-CARE

Many witches work with deities–particularly goddesses from ancient times–to perform their magic. One of the most provocative deities who deserves a self-care shout-out is Lilith: a powerful goddess who reigns over witchcraft, passion, and equality. Her myths can be traced back 5,000 years to ancient Sumer, where she was believed to be a winged wind spirit and priestess of passion. She was later portrayed as Adam's first wife, who left Eden for a free life instead of submitting to inequality. Lilith teaches us to stand up for ourselves rather than being confined to someone else's narrative. I am a devotee of Lilith and wrote extensively about her mythology, archetype, and magic in my book *The GLAM Witch*.

Honoring Our Ancestors

Our ancestors are powerful sources of protection. They are always there as a source of strength and power to tap into and honor. Today's ritual involves creating an ancestral altar and calling upon those who wish us well for guidance and protection.

Photos or belongings of family members who have passed
White candle
Lighter or matches
Offering bowl of water

Fresh flowers
Crystal skull (optional)
Paper
Pen
Cauldron

1. Set up a space devoted to your ancestors. Include photos of them, their belongings, a white candle, a bowl of water, fresh flowers, and a crystal skull (if you have one).

2. Light your white candle. Using your pen and paper, write a letter to your ancestors expressing your love and gratitude for them.

3. Fold your letter and light it on fire using the flame from the candle. Place it in the cauldron and invite your ancestors into your space by saying: "With these words I call upon my ancestors. From blood to blood and bone to bone, I honor those who have come and gone. May those who wish me prosperity and good fortune present themselves to me. Protect and guide me on my continued journey."

4. Commune with your ancestors and pay close attention to any signs you may receive.

5. Maintain your relationship with them by spending time at the altar and offering them something for their blessing and protection every now and then.

Self-Care Cord Magic

Cord magic is a form of folk magic that consists of storing energy in knots. For this spell, we will be tying 9 separate knots in a cord using the following pattern: 1-6-4-7-3-8-5-9-2.

**9-inch cord, in your
favorite color**

1. Hold the cord taut between your hands. Tie knot 1 at the end in your left hand. Focus on your identity and what self-care means to you. As you do this, say: "Knot 1 is for me."

2. Tie knot 2 at the end in your right hand. Focus on how self-care creates balance and equality in your life and say: "Knot 2 is for balance."

3. Tie knot 3 in the middle while focusing on your growth. Say: "Knot 3 is my continued progress."

4. Tie knot 4 between knots 1 and 3. Focus on how self-care is a foundation for your mind, body, and spirit. Say: "Knot 4 is my stability."

5. Tie knot 5 between knots 2 and 3 as you focus on the ways you will take action to ensure your self-care. Say: "Knot 5 is for my actions."

6. Tie knot 6 between knots 1 and 4. Focus on peace of mind and joy. Say: "Knot 6 is finding harmony."

7. Tie knot 7 between knots 3 and 4. Focus on your mental state and say: "Knot 7 is for inner wisdom."

8. Tie knot 8 between knots 3 and 5. Focus on your empowered sense of self. Say: "Knot 8 is for personal power."

9. Tie knot 9 between knots 2 and 5. Focus on the attainment of all of your goals while saying: "Knot 9 is for mastery of me."

10. Keep the cord on your altar, in your pocket, or wear it as a bracelet to further connect with your spiritual self-care. When you feel you have mastered one of the areas, you can untie the corresponding knot.

Crystal Grid for Psychic Power

A crystal grid is a combination of different crystals placed in a formation based on sacred geometry to assist in the manifestation of desired results. Today, let's use the magic of crystals to enhance the psychic power of your spirit.

1 piece labradorite
3 pieces amethyst

3 small selenite wands
Athame or wand (optional)

1. Make space on your altar or shrine, or if space is limited, find another space that will not be disturbed.

2. Place the labradorite crystal in the center of your space. Next, place the amethyst crystals at equal distances around the labradorite. Next, place the selenite wands in the gaps between the amethyst.

3. To activate the grid, hold your activator (the athame or wand, or the index finger of your dominant hand) over the piece of labradorite, focusing on the intention of enhancing your psychic abilities.

4. Trace a line to one of the amethyst pieces and back down to the labradorite. In a clockwise direction, move your activation tool over one of the strands of selenite and back to the labradorite. Continue with this pattern of circulating in and out until you reach the first amethyst.

5. Finalize the grid by moving your activator back to the center labradorite while on your third eye and your psychic intuition building. You can now use the grid for a variety of divination practices.

Psychic Dreams Pillow

Dreams possess important messages and imagery that can provide meaning to our lives. Dream pillows are small cushions to rest on or next to that are stuffed with herbs and crystals and anointed with oils that stimulate vivid dreams and premonitions. We'll be making our own today.

Mugwort tea

2 pieces fabric, cut in 6-inch squares (preferably silver or purple)

Needle and thread

Handful dried chamomile

Handful dried lavender

Handful dried mugwort

Tumbled labradorite crystal

3 drops lavender oil

Journal

Pen

1. Brew a pot of mugwort tea 1 to 2 hours before bedtime to drink as you construct your dream pillow.

2. Position the fabric together so that the outer parts are back-to-back. You will be sewing the pillow inside out and reversing it later.

3. Stich three of the four sides together. Turn the fabric right-side out.

4. Place your herbs and crystal inside the pillow.

5. Fold the raw edges of fabric into the pillow and stitch the open side shut.

6. Place 3 drops of lavender oil on the pillow.

7. Climb into bed and place the pillow under or near your head to help induce prophetic dreams. Just before shutting your eyes, say: "As I lay my head to rest, may I depart on a vision quest. By the power of the herbs and crystal in these seams, I call upon psychic dreams."

8. Drift into a relaxing sleep. Upon waking, write down all the visions you recall in your journal.

Higher Self Tarot Spread

Today, we'll be using a tarot card spread (illustrated on this page) for some divination to understand what areas of growth are needed to ascend in our spirituality.

Tarot deck **Lighter or matches**
Sandalwood incense

1. Light your incense and relax your mind with several deep breaths.

2. Shuffle your deck. As you do, drift out of your current state of mind and ask the universe, ancestors, god/dess, or your version of a higher power to guide you in understanding your spiritual growth.

3. Draw 6 tarot cards and place them as illustrated to interpret the symbolism in each card.

Card 1: represents your current position in the physical world

Card 2: represents the major conflict in your life

Card 3: represents a past situation you have yet to resolve that influences the conflict

Card 4: represents an aspect of your ego that is dragging you down

Card 5: represents your near-future if you continue on your current path

Card 6: represents the recommended approach on how to ascend in your spirituality

Black Coffee Scrying

Scrying is a divination practice that uses a reflective surface for seeing into the dark, subconscious side of things. Witches used to perform scrying by putting mud or ink in water and then looking into black mirrors or obsidian disks. Today, we'll use coffee to do this.

Black coffee   **Mug**

1. Brew your favorite coffee in the morning.

2. Pour your coffee into a mug. Relax and calm your mind as you inhale the aroma.

3. Gaze into the mug at your coffee, seeing your own reflection in the dark mirror.

4. See your shadow self within and visualize merging with your shadow to become whole.

5. Continue visualizing until you see the person who is going to change the world in accordance with your vision.

6. Drink the coffee and savor the taste as you get ready to start your day and embody the vision you saw in your coffee mug.

Connecting with Our Spirit Animals

Spirit animals can come to us in visions, dreams, and meditations with messages to guide us through life. They may show themselves in the physical world or remain a projection of the mind. Either way, spirit animals are powerful allies that have a lot to teach us. Today, we'll be connecting with ours.

Cushion
White candle
Incense

Lighter or matches
Journal
Pen

1. Create a comfortable meditation space with your cushion, candle, and incense. Keep your journal nearby.

2. Close your eyes. Take 10 breaths, inhaling deeply through your nose and exhaling slowly through your mouth. With each breath, visualize that you are in a cave. You can see the light coming through the cave's mouth in the distance. Pay close attention to your surroundings. Call upon the guide that will bring you to the light.

3. In the vision of the cave, imagine that you hear a noise behind you, and turn around. An animal presents itself to you and leads you through the cave.

4. Follow the animal outside the cave, taking note of your surroundings. What time of day is it? What is the environment? What does the animal look like, now that you can see it clearly? Does it look well?

5. Reflect upon your experience once you feel that the meditation is completed. Use the information on the next page to further assist you in interpreting your meditative journey.

SPIRIT ANIMALS

You may encounter many different spirit animals during your lifetime. Sometimes what you are seeing is the mirror of your soul's journey. You may also see a variety of animals—all acting as messengers. Below are some of the more common animals and their associations. I encourage you to supplement this list with your own research.

Bear: represents confidence, protection, and strength
Bee: represents abundance, attraction, and social affairs
Butterfly: represents joy, good fortune, and metamorphosis
Cat: represents adventure, independence, and magic
Crow: represents mystery and trickery
Dog: represents friends and family, loyalty, and playfulness
Fish: represents communication and emotion
Horse: represents freedom, movement, and progress
Hummingbird: represents swift change, happiness, and beauty
Owl: represents intuition and wisdom
Snake: represents fertility, sensuality, and transformation
Spider: represents patience, shadow self, and destiny
Whale: represents imagination and subconscious emotion
Wolf: represents instinct and social interaction

Magical Manifesto

Having gone through the past 12 days tapping into the spiritual side of self-care, let's take a moment to reflect on our belief systems by defining our spirituality and constructing a manifesto for our personal magic.

Sandalwood oil

White or silver candle

Lighter or matches

Journal

Pen

1. Anoint your candle with 3 drops of sandalwood oil.

2. Light the candle.

3. Use your journal to write down your spiritual truths by the light of the candle. To help in your writing, consider the following:

   - What are your core beliefs and how do you define your practice?

   - What is your personal code of conduct? What are your values?

   - In what way does nature provide sustenance to your practice?

   - Do you have a deity or spirit guide that you are devoted to?

   - Is there a particular type of magic that you focus on?

   - What are your inspirations?

   - What are your spiritual goals?

4. Hold your journal and repeat these words once you have written your manifesto: "By the words written here, I define my spirituality as (read your manifesto aloud). In perfect love, and perfect trust I, (your name), dedicate myself to my spiritual truth and the universal forces of magic!"

5. Kiss the pages as a symbolic act. You may either remove the pages from the journal and place them on your altar as a reminder of your spiritual credo or leave them in your magical journal to refer back to.

Ritual of Gratitude

Rituals of gratitude are a powerful expression to the universe, your deities, ancestors, and spirit guides that you are appreciative of the blessings they have bestowed on you. These blessings may be wonderful rewards or obstacles meant to challenge you and help you grow. Regardless, by offering your thanks, you become a magnet to pull in more of what serves you.

1 piece of paper
Pen
Shovel or digging tool
1 quartz crystal point

1 fresh white rose
1 (187-milliliter) bottle
or 1 glass of champagne
or prosecco*

Use lemonade for a nonalcoholic alternative.

1. Find a peaceful and private location outdoors where you feel safe—a garden, backyard, public park, etc.

2. Reflect on all that you are grateful for—all the lessons you have learned up until now and all the wonder yet to come. Write this down on your sheet of paper and fold the paper four times.

3. Dig a hole and place the paper inside with the crystal on top, pointing up.

4. Re-cover the hole with the expelled dirt.

5. Stick the stem of the rose into the dirt.

6. Raise your glass to the sky, close your eyes, and freely profess your gratitude.

7. Have a sip of the libation and pour the remaining liquid in a clockwise circle around the rose.

The Essence of Magic: A Meditation

Congratulations! We are halfway through our 90 days. How does it feel? Considering that we are at the center of our journey, let's embrace a vivid meditation on the essence of magic.

Raw rock salt
1 green candle
1 yellow candle
1 red candle

1 blue candle
Lighter or matches
Cushion

1. Create a circle of salt large enough to sit in.

2. Anchor the circle with a candle at each of the cardinal directions (green in the north, yellow in the east, red in the south, and blue in the west).

3. Light the candles and sit on the cushion in the center of the circle.

4. Close your eyes. Take 10 breaths, inhaling deeply through your nose and exhaling slowly through your mouth. With each breath, begin to descend from your current state and visualize a sphere of light swirling around you.

5. Feel all the powers of the universe flowing through you as you float in a giant sphere of sparkling light. Remember, will is the key that sets your intention free.

6. Breathe, believe, and receive the magic of this moment as it pulsates through you from between the worlds. Reflect upon all that you have learned and achieved in your magical self-care leading up to this moment. Know that as you keep practicing, the magic of you will only continue to blossom.

7. When you feel the pull back to consciousness, visualize the sphere beginning to disappear from around you.

8. Open your eyes, take a bow, blow out your candles, and continue on your journey.

ENVIRONMENT

Home Cleanse and Clear Ritual

Whether you are a minimalist or a maximalist, a clean home is a happy home. Cleaning your space shows respect for yourself and your belongings. It can also be seen as a ritualistic process that helps clear the mind, energize the body, and cleanse your soul. Therefore, today's exercise is a home cleanse.

White candle

Lemon oil

Lighter or matches

4 pieces clear quartz crystal

Bags or boxes

Sage smudging wand or palo santo stick

Feather (optional)

1. Anoint the white candle with lemon oil to infuse cleansing energy into your space. Light the candle.

2. Hold the 4 quartz crystals in your hand, saying: "Clearest crystals, help keep my house sparkling clean."

3. Place a quartz crystal in each of the outer corners that make up the floor plan of your entire home.

4. Clean and tidy your space. Place unwanted items in bags or boxes to be donated.

5. As you clean, think about how the physical cleaning of your space mirrors the internal, emotional cleaning you have been doing.

6. Light your smudging wand or palo santo stick and walk around your home once you've finished cleaning. Blow the smoke into your space or fan it out with a feather. While doing this, chant: "Cleansed and cleared, my personal place is now a sacred space."

Happy Home Mist

Now that you have cleansed and cleared your space, it is time to attract happiness into it. The homemade spray we'll be making today is a magical air freshener to harmonize good vibes and happiness at home.

1 (4-ounce) clear spray bottle
2½ ounces distilled water
¼ ounce alcohol
10 drops orange oil,
  for happiness
10 drops rose oil, to attract joy

5 drops sandalwood oil,
  for spirituality
Tumbled amethyst, for peace
  (small enough to fit in
  the bottle)

1. In the spray bottle, combine the distilled water, alcohol, orange oil, rose oil, sandalwood oil, and tumbled amethyst. As you add each ingredient, speak to it directly and tell it what its purpose is, as defined in the materials list.

2. Seal the bottle and shake it vigorously, saying: "Energies combine to manifest happiness in this home of mine."

3. Leave the bottle sitting under the sunlight a few hours to collect the warm and loving energies of the sun.

4. Shake up the potion again before misting your home as you chant: "Through these tiny pearls of mist, I conjure a home of bliss."

Honoring the Spirit of Place

The land on which we live is a spirit, and each location has its own guardian. Today, we'll honor the spirit of place in our homes as an act of gratitude.

Comfortable shoes   **Backpack or bag**

1. Dress comfortably for a nature walk and grab a backpack or other bag to collect objects on your way.

2. Gather a selection of rocks, sticks, flowers, leaves, feathers, or other natural items to which you are drawn.

3. Find a location during your stroll where you can construct a mini altar out of your findings in honor of the spirit of place.

4. Create a pentagram star out of the sticks on the ground. Secure the symbol in place by pushing the sticks a bit into the dirt.

5. Decorate around the pentagram with the items you've gathered. You can place stones around the star, making it a pentacle, or layer them directly in the center of the star.

6. Call upon the spirits of the land and let them know that your offering is in honor of them. Say: "I honor the spirits of this land. A land set outside time and space. I offer my gratitude and respect to you, so that you may prosper in this place."

Moonbathing

Moonbathing is the practice of lying or sitting under the light of the moon to tap into the lunar energy. This spell combines the practice with a sacred bathing ritual to further experience the power of the moon.

Epsom salt

1 white rose

4 drops gardenia oil

4 drops jasmine oil

4 drops rose oil

White candle

Lighter or matches

Journal

Pen

Robe (optional)

1. Draw a warm bath in the evening.

2. Add a handful of Epsom salts, the petals from a white rose, and 4 drops each of gardenia, jasmine, and rose oils to the water.

3. Bathe in the water for as long as feels right.

4. Drain the bath and lightly dry yourself so that you are still slightly wet, anointed from your lunar bath.

5. Dress in a robe or remain unclothed if you are comfortable.

6. Go to a window where you can see the moon, or go outside if you have a private backyard, and let yourself be illuminated by the lunar light.*

7. Reflect on how the current phase of the moon mirrors your self-care journey while receiving the moon's energy. Use the descriptions of lunar phases on pages 31 and 32.

8. Record any thoughts, feelings, or emotions in your journal.

It is preferable to be visually under the moon, but if that's not feasible or if the moon is not visible, visualize yourself being saturated with moonlight.

DRAWING DOWN THE MOON

Drawing down the moon is a popular ceremony that is performed on the night of the full moon. The moon is often seen as a representation of the goddess energy. In traditional covens, the high priestess embodies this energy and disperses it among the rest of the coven members. However, you do not have to be in a coven to perform this ritual. On the next full moon, follow the circle casting template provided on page 42. During the heart of the ritual, read a personal invocation that you have prepared, a lunar poem, or the *Charge of the Goddess* (the most popular invocation for drawing down the moon). With your arms outstretched, call down the lunar essence into you. Follow with meditation. Record your experiences in your journal and then close the circle.

Soak Up the Sun

The sun is a powerful source of spiritual and physical energy to all organisms on Earth—including us. It is recommended that we get 10 to 20 minutes of direct natural sunlight every 3 to 5 days to absorb vitamin D. Today, we'll be doing just that through a sun-bathing ritual for sustenance.

**Cushion, mat, or other
  comfortable padding**

1. Find a natural area where you will be touched by the sun's rays. If your home gets a lot of natural sunlight, you can set up a place inside. Otherwise, venture outside to a space where you won't be disturbed.

2. Sit, lie back, or stretch out into a comfortable position on a cushion, mat, or other comfortable surface.

3. Close your eyes and feel the warmth of the sun shine down on you. As you do this, visualize the pulsating flames of the sun. Think about how we benefit from it—how it affects our crops, the plants and flowers, and the overall sustainability of our planet. Think about how right now, in this moment, your cells are being recharged by its powerful light while you breathe slowly and deeply.

4. Do this for about 15 minutes. Upon completion, bow in respect to the sun and express your gratitude for the energy that it has provided you.

Stargazing

This exercise combines environmental observation with some techno witchery to enjoy the beauty of the stars. Remember that the witch's symbol is the star, and stars are all around us, a constant reminder that we exist in an expansive universe. For this exercise, use a stargazing app such as SkySafari. I like to use this app even if I have a clear view of the stars, for help determining the constellations and planets. Apps like SkySafari have a compass option to see the location of planetary objects in real-time.

Smartphone with a **Journal**
  stargazing app **Pen**

1. Go outdoors with your smartphone in hand and try to find the clearest possible view of the sky above.

2. As you observe the stars naturally or through a stargazing app, think about how our sun is a star and that each of the stars in the sky is another sun in another solar system light years away. In fact, the light that you are seeing right now is actually millions of years old.

3. Become aware of how you are only one small piece of a greater whole that is infinite. Right now, in this moment, all time is here, and all power is now.

4. If you are using an app, click on any stars that stand out to you and learn more about them.

5. Write about your observations and feelings in your journal.

Tree Meditation

One of the best ways to connect to the environment is to bond with the four elements—earth, air, fire, and water. First up is earth—the element of structure, form, and stability. This exercise involves venturing outside to perform a tree meditation and become more grounded with the world in front of you, beneath you, and around you.

Tree   **Cushion or blanket (optional)**

1. Head outside and locate a tree in a private, safe, and undisturbed location that you feel drawn to.

2. Place the cushion at the base of the tree and sit so that your back is resting against the trunk.

3. Ground and center yourself. Close your eyes and take 10 breaths, inhaling deeply through your nose and exhaling slowly through your mouth. With each breath, visualize yourself sinking into and merging with the tree.

4. Feel yourself becoming symbiotic with the tree. Visualize its roots reaching down into the earth, providing stability and sustainability for the tree. Feel the breeze pushing against the branches and leaves. Think about how the sunlight is absorbed through the leaves to provide it with energy. Ask yourself, "How does the tree care for itself and all of its various parts? How does it remain in a state of tranquility regardless of what is happening around it?"

5. Reflect on how your life mirrors the tree and how your self-care gives you a similar stability.

6. Bow in gratitude and reverence to the tree for its assistance in your meditation.

Air Incense Blend

Today, we will focus our magical self-care efforts on connecting to the element of air by creating an incense blend and reflecting on how this sacred element has impacted our self-care journeys.

Mortar and pestle
2 parts benzoin resin
1 part crushed palo santo wood
1 part dried lemongrass
Screened charcoal burner or
  fireproof metal bowl filled
  with sand or salt

Tongs
Charcoal disc
Lighter or matches
Feather (optional)

1. Use a mortar and pestle to grind the benzoin, palo santo, and lemongrass as fine as possible.

2. Sit in a comfortable position on the floor or at a table. Place your charcoal burner or metal bowl in front of you.

3. Use the tongs to place the charcoal disc onto the burner (or metal bowl filled with sand or salt). It should be in a concave position so that your ingredients can be added to it.

4. Light the charcoal until it sparks.

5. Add a pinch of your incense blend to the hot charcoal disc once the charcoal has developed a ring of ash around it.

6. Use a feather or your hand to fan the smoke in your direction. Breathe it in and contemplate the miraculous power of air. Feel the oxygen in your lungs and smell the scent of the sacred herbs. Air is associated with imagination, intellect, and communication. Reflect on what parts of your life act as the air to your self-care.

7. Scrape off the ashes and add more if you wish once your incense has charged. The disc will burn for about an hour.

Campfire Meditation

Fire is a powerful source of transformation, creation, and warmth. Today, we'll connect to this element through a full-sensory meditation.

Campfire audio   **Lighter or matches**

Laptop, radio, or phone   **Pillow or cushion**

10 red tea light candles

1. Play your campfire audio track.

2. Create a circle on the floor that is big enough to freely move in, using the 10 tea lights as a barrier. (White tea lights will do if red ones are unavailable.)

3. Light the tea lights and darken the room. Sit in a comfortable position on your pillow or cushion in the center of the circle.

4. Close your eyes. Take 10 breaths, inhaling deeply through your nose and exhaling slowly through your mouth. Listen closely to the sound of the fire playing from your audio device.

5. Focus on the creative element of fire that surrounds you and how, even with your eyes shut, you can still make out a soft glow. Think about the hot molten core of our planet, the burning sun that shines down on us, and the heat of your heart. You may even begin to sway from side to side, mimicking the flickering of the flames around you. Reflect on how your creative potential has transformed throughout your self-care journey.

6. End your meditation and blow out the candles whenever it feels right. As the flame turns to smoke, remain conscious of fire's continued transformation into ether.

Shungite Water Ritual

Today's ritual focuses on the hydrating element of water. We'll be purifying and amplifying the water in this ritual with a piece of elite shungite. When placed in water, shungite neutralizes any contaminants, making the water a pure drinking source. This is because it contains carbon molecules called fullerenes. Elite shungite can be easily purchased online.

Elite shungite crystal **Pitcher**
Saucepan **Water**

1. Sterilize the shungite the night before performing this ritual by placing it in a saucepan of boiling water. Allow it to boil for 10 minutes, and then remove it from the saucepan and let cool. Discard the water.

2. Rinse the shungite in cool water once it has cooled down. Do not use soap.

3. Dry off the stone and place it into a pitcher of water. Place the pitcher, uncovered, in your refrigerator overnight for at least 12 hours.

4. Create a relaxing environment and pour yourself a glass of water from the pitcher that contains the shungite. As you do, feel the water flowing through your body. Consider that 60 percent of your body and 71 percent of Earth is made of water. Visualize the streams, rivers, and oceans of the world and see their liquid current make waves within your soul. Focus on the emotional aspect of water and how it connects to compassion, love, and forgiveness.

5. Aim to drink the remainder of the pitcher over the course of the day with this same sense of mindfulness.

Observing the Seasonal Shifts

Depending on your geographical location, you may or may not experience a rich transition between the four seasons of spring, summer, fall, and winter. For this ritual, we'll observe the current season and how it mirrors our own magical self-care journeys.

1. Find a quiet place in nature. Use the actions below depending on what season your region is experiencing:

   - **Spring:** Observe the rebirth of the land. Now is a time when flowers, trees, and other greenery begin to bloom. Pick the bud of a flower or tree and bring it back to your altar to celebrate the renewal of the season.

   - **Summer:** Observe the heat and warm weather. This warmth provides nourishment to all organisms and is a representation of life itself. Pick a flower and place it in a vase on your altar in honor of the season that represents the act of coming into full bloom.

   - **Fall:** Observe how nature's vitality begins to fade. It is a time for harvest and cultivating the bounty that summer has brought. Pick up a fallen leaf or branch and bring it back to your altar to represent the harvesting that occurs before the death of land in the winter.

   - **Winter:** Observe the death of the land. If snow is on the ground, gather a bit and place it in a bowl. Leave it on your altar to melt and evaporate, representing the transformation of seasons. Alternatively, collect a pine cone, acorn, or any other winter-themed item found in nature.

Magical Foraging

Magical foraging is a wonderful way to connect with nature while sourcing tools and ingredients from their natural habitat. If you reside in a suburban or rural area, you may wish to access a forest preserve or field to do your foraging and will likely come across different branches, stones, flowers, or other foliage. City witches can forage in their concrete jungle by finding flowers or greenery in parks and discarded items on the streets or in alleys that speak to their magical needs, such as playing cards or antiques.

Comfortable shoes **Quartz crystal**
Backpack or bag

1. Dress comfortably and grab a backpack or bag so that you have a place to store your finds.

2. Grasp a quartz crystal in both hands and enchant it by saying: "Crystal clear, enhance my vision. Guide me to what I need."

3. Place the crystal in your pocket. Go out on your journey and allow yourself to be pulled in whatever direction the universe, and your crystal, guides you.

4. Keep your eyes peeled for signs, synchronicity, and any items that jump out at you. Collect anything that stands out to you.

5. Bring your item(s) home and place them on your altar.

6. Reflect on each item you gathered and how it mirrors what is going on in your life. How can you learn from it? Let it teach you.

Animal Observation

Observing the animals that live in our natural environment is a great way to connect with nature. For example, animals are known to display unusual behavior as storms approach. We don't really need any materials for this magical exercise, but the list below has some optional items that can be used to enhance the experience. Remember to be safe while observing wild animals and avoid trampling their environment.

Binoculars (optional)
Sketchpad or journal (optional)
Pen (optional)

Smartphone or camera (optional)

1. Head out into nature.

2. Sit in a safe, comfortable space and observe your surroundings. Perhaps it is peaceful, or maybe it is loud and chaotic. Look for an animal to guide you.

3. Pay attention to how it behaves. Is it nervous or calm? Is it moving fast or slowly? Is it being loud or sly? How is it interacting in its environment?

4. Draw the animals as you observe them or snap photos to reflect on later.

5. Try some animal-led divination, if you'd like, to get answers to questions that may be on your mind. For instance, if a bird presents itself to you, ask a question; if you hear one chirp the answer is "no," two chirps "yes," and three or more means that you should ask again later.

Witchy Window Garden

Gardening is a therapeutic activity that allows us to forge a deeper connection with nature. Many witches have magical gardens where they harvest their herbs for spellwork and eating. More advanced green witches may wish to perform this spell using seeds rather than fresh specimens.

5 fresh herbs (such as basil, lavender, rosemary, sage, or thyme)

5 pieces clear quartz

Bowl

Water

Newspaper

Large pot or planter's box

Soil

Gloves (optional)

Shovel (optional)

1. Gather a selection of 5 different herbs. Ideally, the herbs should be associated with magic that you wish to bring into your space, or a theme that is relevant in your magical practice. Refer back to page 35 for some examples of herbal magic correlations.

2. Place 5 quartz crystals into a bowl of water and place the bowl directly in sunlight in the space you intend to set up your garden. Enchant the crystals by holding the bowl up to the sun and drawing in its vitality by saying: "Magic crystal, absorb this solar vitality!"

3. For easy cleanup, lay down several sheets of newspaper on the flat surface on which you chose to pot your plants.

4. Transfer the herbs into your pot or planter's box, along with additional soil.

5. Bury one of each of the crystals at the base of each plant.

6. Use the leftover water to water the plants while chanting "grow."

7. Continue to look after your plants. Enjoy growing and harvesting your herbs for magical purposes.

Reduce Our Magical Footprint

We are responsible for our planet—it is our home. Because witches honor nature as sacred, we have an even bigger responsibility to help save Earth than most. This evening, save some energy and create a magical, natural environment with candlelight to relax in.

5 to 10 candles
Incense
Lighter or matches

Books, journals, pens, art supplies, or other creative activities
Fresh organic snacks (fruits, vegetables, or nuts)

1. Reduce your electrical usage by lighting candles around the house in the evening rather than using electricity. Be sure to practice fire safety: Do not place the candles in any location that could easily catch fire or pose a risk.

2. Light your favorite incense to create an aromatic, witchy atmosphere.

3. Relax, meditate, read a book by candlelight, journal, draw, paint, do yoga, or whatever your witchy heart wishes. Snack on fresh organic fruits, veggies, and nuts. As you do this, remain cognizant of how even this small little step is helping our planet.

4. Make this as much of a regular habit as possible.

RELATIONSHIPS
&
COMMUNITY

Bless a Local Business

Interacting with local businesses provides a great intersection between our environment and relationships with our communities. Today, we will extend our healing witch powers to bless a local business with good fortune.

Knife	**Pinch dried catnip**
White chime candle*	**Pinch ground black pepper**
4 drops orange oil	**Lighter or matches**
Small bowl	**Small bag**

1. Identify the local business that you wish to bless.

2. Carve the business's name into the white candle.

3. Anoint the candle with orange oil to stimulate prosperity and stability.

4. Use a small bowl to evenly mix a pinch of catnip to amplify attraction and black pepper for protection. Sprinkle the mixture evenly onto the freshly anointed candle.

5. Light the candle and say the following while visualizing the business's success: "It is my will from love and power that I do bless (name of the business) on this magic hour. Prosperous, safe, and happy for the good of all, blessed be!"

6. Let the candle safely burn out. Place any remnants of wax and herbs into a small bag and sprinkle them on the grounds of the business.

*Chime candles have a burn time of 2 to 2½ hours. Please allow enough time to let this candle burn out completely under watchful supervision.

The Cord of Friendship

This is a simple cord spell to attract friendship. It can either help bind us to our covens or help attract new friendships. A witch's ladder is a magical charm created by knotting or braiding cord with a specific intention. The particular weaving pattern we are doing is called a butterfly stitch. Online tutorials demonstrating the stitch may be helpful. The most suitable colors for this are pink and orange, but you may also substitute your favorite colors or any others that possess meaning to you.

**2 pieces (30-inch) cord, in the
colors of your choosing**

1. Hold the two cords evenly and make a knot at the top.

2. Make a loop at the base of the knot using one of the cords.

3. Take the other cord and go around the loop with it. Make another loop through the opening of the first cord.

4. Pull down on the first cord so that it tightens the cord in place.

5. Create a new loop with the first cord by inserting it through the opening of the second cord. Pull down on the second cord.

6. Repeat steps 3 though 5 until your cords are braided in place. As you braid the two cords, focus intently on your friends, how meaningful those friendships are, and how happy they make you feel.

7. Knot the end of your cord. You can add the finished cord to your keychain, wear it as jewelry, or carry it on your person when interacting with friends.

Greeting Card Spell

Because of technology, hardly anyone sends physical, handwritten cards anymore. Well, today, we will! This is a simple and sweet spell for sending happiness and love to a friend, family member, mentor, lover, or any person to whom we feel naturally drawn.

Blank greeting card
Pen
Envelope
Stamp

Rose quartz crystal
Rose incense stick
Lighter or matches

1. Select a blank greeting card with a design that calls to you.

2. Hold the card to your heart as you look out your window to the sunrise. Think about the warmth that your intended recipient has brought to your life.

3. Write out a nice note expressing how happy and grateful you are for what the recipient of your card adds to your life.

4. Seal the envelope, address it, and stamp it. Place it in the center of your altar and place a rose quartz on top of it.

5. Light the incense and use it to trace the following symbols over the card and crystal:

   Heart: for love

   Cross: for the intersection of partnership

   Pentagram: for magic

6. Say aloud: "I am thankful for (<u>name of individual</u>), my (<u>their role in your life</u>). I bless our companionship with my love, partnership, and magic, and hope this magical message will bring them joy. From my heart to theirs, so mote it be."

7. Kiss the card three times before mailing it out.

Accepting Help

A past letdown or the need to be in control can keep us from asking for help. Feathers are representative of air, which rules thought patterns and communication. They are also exceptionally light and can be easy to blow away. This simple spell uses a lone feather to help us release whatever is holding us back from finding solidarity in others.

Natural feather

1. Go outside at sunrise with a feather in hand.

2. Face the rising sun while holding the feather in your dominant hand by pinching its end with your index finger and thumb. Extend your arm out in front of you.

3. Close your eyes. Channel all that you feel is holding you back in your life into the feather, whether that's fear, resentment, stubbornness, or all those things.

4. Say: "I surrender all control and welcome the help of others."

5. Loosen your grip on the feather and exhale with force, pushing the feather out of your hands and into the wind.

6. Watch it drift away as a symbolic and magical representation of that blockage within yourself being freed.

7. Be proactive and ask for or accept the help of others throughout your day.

MAGICAL ACTIVISM

In his book *Apocalyptic Witchcraft*, Peter Grey states, "If the land is poisoned, the witchcraft must respond." We are currently living in challenging times where resources and freedoms are not being distributed equally. Magical activism is a responsibility. We must use our voices to help humanity end inequality and injustice. While fighting against racism, homophobia, sexism, and all other injustices, remember to start by acting practically and following up with your magic. Below are some tips for engaging in magical activism:

→ Talk less and listen more to those who are directly impacted by injustice.
→ Allow marginalized individuals to be heard.
→ Educate yourself on social justice matters.
→ Check your privileges.
→ Use your voice and any privilege you possess to amplify and help the cause.

Support Social Justice

Today, we'll support a social justice initiative by performing this spell on behalf of any organization of our choosing. The goal of this spell is to offer the organization protection and increase the good it does in the world.

Computer and printer or paper
Pen
Justice tarot card
Salt
Orange chime candle
  and holder

Black pepper oil
Pinch ground cayenne pepper
Lighter or matches

1. Select a social justice organization that appeals to you.

2. Print out an image of the organization's logo or write the name of the organization on a piece of paper. Draw a pentacle over the logo or name with a pen.

3. Place the logo or name on top of the justice tarot card.

4. Use salt to create a circle around the card in a clockwise motion while chanting "protect" until the circle has been looped closed.

5. Anoint the candle with 3 drops of black pepper oil to bring protection and banish ill will.

6. Rub a bit of cayenne pepper on the candle to repel negativity and speed up results.

7. Place the candle in a holder on top of the card and paper. Light the candle and say: "I call forth the power of justice. With this flame may you burn bright, to help (<u>name of the organization</u>) do what is right. Protect them as they fight for change."

8. Visualize the organization having successful outcomes.

Purification Bath

No matter how positive we are, there will always be individuals who act negatively toward us. This spell is an all-around protection bath designed to cleanse, clear, and empower our energy while shielding us from the unnecessary toxicity of others.

Knife	**Star anise**
Black chime candle and holder	**10 drops lemon oil**
Pine oil	**Tumbled obsidian crystal**
Mixing bowl	**Lighter or matches**
3 tablespoons black lava salt	**Frankincense incense**
1 teaspoon dried rosemary	**Lighter or matches**

1. Use the knife to carve your first name into one side of the candle and the word "negativity" into the other side. Chip away at the bottom of the candle until the wick is exposed.

2. Anoint the candle with a drop of pine oil for protection.

3. Draw a warm bath.

4. Use a mixing bowl to combine the black lava salt, rosemary, and star anise. Add this mixture to the bathwater.

5. Add 10 drops of lemon oil to the bathwater, along with the black obsidian.

6. Dim the lights and light the candle and frankincense incense.

7. State: "By the power of fire, may negativity retire. I purify myself tonight, by the transformative power of your light."

8. Climb into the bath. Fully submerge yourself at least once. Visualize any negativity washing off you.

9. Release the bathtub drain after about 30 minutes and stay in the tub until all the water has drained out. Visualize all the negativity going down the drain.

10. Allow the candle to continue to safely burn until extinguished.

Office Optimism Spray

A positive work environment promotes teamwork, morale, and peace. The recipe that follows is for an aromatic potion to help foster optimism in your office space.

1 (4-ounce) spray bottle
6 tablespoons water
2 ounces unscented witch hazel
7 drops mint oil

7 drops lemongrass oil
Tumbled aquamarine, for communication (small enough to fit in the bottle)

1. In the spray bottle, mix the water and witch hazel, swirling in a clockwise motion while visualizing a positive work environment fueled by teamwork.

2. Add the mint oil, which is known to invigorate communication and reinforce positive energy, and the lemongrass oil.

3. Say: "Magical mint and lemongrass, assist me to induce optimistic teamwork evenly."

4. Hold the tumbled aquamarine in your receptive hand. Make a fist around it while intending that it help instill cooperation in your workplace. Say: "Aquamarine, open doors for communication to flow freely."

5. Add the aquamarine to the bottle, close it, and give it a gentle shake.

6. Mist the air while saying: "May the energies of herbs, minerals, and waters combine with this optimistic intention of mine. With each spray, may teamwork grow, and positivity stay."

7. Repeat the last step as needed.

Mind My Business Spell

Whether it's casual banter between friends, water cooler chat at the office, or social media sharing, we are constantly trading information and ideas, some of which may not be factual. Let's use a freezer spell to encourage ourselves to say less and do more, reducing our participation in gossip.

Strip of black paper
Black pen
1 plastic bag or container

Garlic clove or pinch
  garlic powder
Water

1. Write your name backward on a piece of paper.

2. Over your name, write the words "I mind my business."

3. Place the paper into the bag or container, along with the garlic, which is a powerful banishing agent.

4. Pour water over the garlic and paper.

5. Seal the bag or container and shake it in a counterclockwise circle to stimulate banishing energy while saying: "I banish gossip from my lips and vow to stop needless quips. For the good of all, especially me, it is my will; so shall it be."

6. Place the bag or container in your freezer.

7. Remove the item from the freezer and discard it after a month has passed.

Better Communication Meditation

Having done the work to purge unsavory words from our lips yesterday, today we will do a meditation spell to stimulate better communication so that we can be of greater service in our relationships and community.

Yoga mat or cushion

Blue candle

Lighter or matches

Sandalwood incense

Amazonite crystal

1. Set up your space with a yoga mat or other comfortable cushion to lie on.

2. Light a blue candle and position it so that it is 6 to 12 inches above where your head will rest while you are on your back. Light the incense and place it nearby.

3. Holding the amazonite crystal in your right hand, lie down on the mat. Inhale deeply through your nostrils and exhale slowly from your mouth.

4. Place the amazonite crystal on your throat. Amazonite is a powerful crystal known for enhancing communication on all levels.

5. Visualize a flowing blue cloud of light stream from the crystal, wrapping itself gently around your neck. Imagine it passing through your skin and creating a glowing ball of blue light in your throat.

6. Begin to hum lightly, focusing your intent on opening up channels of communication. Picture yourself expressing your opinions and compromising with others.

7. See the light fade away when you feel pulled back to consciousness. Grab the crystal off your throat before sitting up.

8. Carry the crystal whenever you feel you could benefit from an extra zap of communication energy.

Harmony Rose Potion

Roses are one of the most magical flowers, associated with love and healing. Witches can use them as an all-purpose plant. Today, we'll create a special tea potion to foster harmony with those who cross our paths.

2 cups water

Small saucepan

2 tablespoons dried organic
  rose petals

Colander or straining device

Mug

Honey

Spoon

Ice (optional)

1. Focus your intentions on creating harmony with others as you pour 2 cups of water into a small saucepan and bring it to a boil.

2. Add the rose petals to the water and reduce the heat to a simmer for 5 to 10 minutes.

3. Use a colander or other straining device to pour the liquid into a mug.

4. Add a dollop of honey and stir with a spoon in a clockwise motion until the honey is dissolved.

5. Drink the tea warm or allow it to cool and serve over ice. As you sip the potion, feel its energies radiate through your body, helping you become a beacon of loving, harmonizing energy.

Setting Boundaries

Setting boundaries between ourselves and others is a way to exercise self-care by taking your needs into consideration. Boundaries prevent us from being taken advantage of or doing too much. Today, we'll set a magical boundary.

Photo of yourself	**Piece of paper**
4 pieces smoky quartz	**Scissors**
Gray chime candle and holder	**Pen**
Lighter or matches	**Salt**

1. Place a photo of yourself on your altar or workspace.

2. Put a piece of smoky quartz 1 inch from each of the photo's four corners.

3. Set the gray candle on top of the photo in a holder. Light the candle.

4. Use a sheet of paper to write down the different individuals and situations in your life for which you wish to create a boundary. Cut each of these out into a smaller piece of paper.

5. Write out specifically what your boundary is on the other sides of the pieces of paper.

6. Scatter the strips of paper around your photo and the crystals.

7. Draw a line of salt from one crystal to the next in a clockwise rotation. While doing this, say: "The sacred salt has been cast. My wall is up, you may not pass. I exercise my right to create this boundary. By the power of my will, so shall it be."

8. Allow the candle to burn out and leave the materials on your altar until you feel as though the spell has taken effect. Upon that time, bury the crystals, photo, and salt remains in the earth to ground its energy.

Social Media Detox

Social media is a wonderful way to stay connected to friends and family and extend our networks. However, electronic addiction, desensitization to the natural world, comparison syndrome, regurgitation of false information, and petty arguments can impact our minds, bodies, and spirits. Today's spell promotes a social media detox.

Pen　　　　　　　　　　　**Large smoky quartz crystal**
Piece of paper　　　　　　**4 clear quartz crystals**

1. Go to your altar or another workspace upon waking up. Write down the different social media platforms you have accounts with and the URLs for each of them on a piece of paper.

2. Fold the paper four times and place it in the center of the workspace.

3. Place the smoky quartz on top of the paper.

4. Anchor the corners of the paper by placing a clear quartz point on each one.

5. Place your right hand on the smoky quartz, close your eyes, and repeat these words: "I detox myself from the frequency of social media toxicity. Smoky quartz, ground my energy so that I can disengage healthily."

6. Go into your smartphone and turn off the notifications from or uninstall your social media platforms for the day to reduce temptation. Do not log back on for at least 24 hours.

7. Make note of your productivity levels without social media taking up time.

Give Back

One way to stimulate care within your community is through kindness. Today's goal is to give something of value to someone else. An incense or oil blend, any amount of money to an organization or cause you're passionate about, an extra-large tip at a restaurant, or a work of art are just some ideas.

**Any valued item of
your choosing**

1. Select an individual or organization to bestow a gift on, as well as what you wish to give.

2. Enchant your gift in a way that feels right to you while visualizing the happiness it will bring.

3. Deliver the gift to the intended recipient in whatever way feels right to you.

WITCH WAR

Witch wars are toxic arguments that traditionally happen between conflicting witches on social media. However, the idea can extend beyond the magical community to your interactions with other individuals. When situations like this happen, it can be very tempting to immediately respond back or try to defend yourself. But disengaging is a better strategy. Disengaging is a power play that allows you to win by default by removing yourself from the situation.

Rose Quartz Meditation

Rose quartz is the universal crystal for love and healing. It is a wonderful crystal for self-care because it helps intensify your sense of self-love, self-worth, and self-compassion. Today, we'll connect with this loving crystal to access its tenderness.

Cushion

Pink candle (optional)

Rose incense (optional)

Lighter or matches (optional)

Rose quartz crystal

1. Sit in a comfortable position on your cushion and light a pink candle and/or rose incense to further intensify the energies of the rose quartz, if you'd like.

2. Hold a piece of rose quartz in your hands. Close your eyes and take 10 breaths, inhaling deeply through your nose and exhaling slowly through your mouth. With each breath, feel yourself drift into a state of supreme peace.

3. Visualize a light, dusty rose–colored light softly materializing around you as you hold the stone. See it intensifying into a bright, light-pink tone that pours into your heart.

4. Focus on your emotions, how your emotions are impacted by others, and how they influence your actions, which in turn affect others. How can you be more empathetic? Think about how you can tenderly touch those around you with the power of love.

5. Visualize the light slowly start to fade when you feel your meditation is complete. Take another 10 deep, slow breaths, and come back into reality. Carry the crystal with you for the day.

Reflecting Love Spell

This reflective love spell can be performed whether or not we have a romantic partner. It's meant to help us attract love by honoring the qualities we long for in ourselves.

Mortar and pestle	3 drops rose oil
Dried hibiscus	Compact mirror
Dried rose petals	Lighter or matches
Knife	Paper and pen
Vanilla bean	Cauldron or fireproof bowl
1 red chime candle	

1. Use a mortar and pestle to grind the hibiscus and rose petals into a fine powder.

2. Use a knife to slit the vanilla bean down its shaft. Using the edge of the knife, push the aromatic powder into the mortar and pestle and stir clockwise.

3. Carve a heart into the candle. In the center of the heart, carve your initials. Lick your thumb and slide it over your carved initials to seal them with your essence.

4. Anoint the candle with rose oil.

5. Rub the powder all over it so that it is completely dusted.

6. Open your compact mirror and place it on a flat surface. Using the lighter or a match, warm the bottom of the candle so that it is slightly melted.

7. Place the candle bottom on the center of the mirror and apply a little pressure to help it stick to the mirror's surface.

8. Light the candle.

9. Write a list of all the nonphysical characteristics you desire in a partner, whether you are single or not, using the candlelight to illuminate your writing surface.

CONTINUED >

10. Read your list aloud and then safely light the paper on fire using the candle's flame. Place the burning paper into the cauldron or fireproof bowl.

11. Stare into the flame and focus on how you can emulate all the qualities of your desired partner in yourself, so that you can become a mirror to attract those traits in a lover.

12. Let the candle burn completely and safely. Remove the candle, close the compact, and store them in a safe place.

PROSPERITY
&
SUCCESS

A Future Forecast

Let us now transition our self-care journey into the theme of prosperity and success. We'll begin by performing a bit of divination to uncover what our futures hold if we continue on our current paths.

Tarot deck

Book or other resource on tarot meanings (optional, if you are a beginner)

Journal

Pen

1. Shuffle the tarot deck. As you do, drift out of your current state of mind and ask the universe, ancestors, god/dess, or your version of a higher power what the next 12 months look like for you on your current path.

2. Draw 4 cards and place them faceup in a row from left to right. Draw 2 additional rows in the same fashion. In the end, you will have 3 rows with 4 columns. Draw one last card and place it beneath the 3 rows. You will have 13 cards. Use the diagram on page 157 as a guide.

3. Interpret card 1, which represents the themes and prevailing energies of the current month. The remaining cards indicate each subsequent month for the upcoming year.

4. Interpret card 13, which represents the combined theme of the year to come if you continue on your current path.

5. Reflect upon your spread and record your findings in a journal. Spend some time creating an action plan of how you will move forward in the year to come to maximize your success with self-care.

6. Place card 13 on your altar to use in the next spell.

1

2

3

4

5

6

7

8

9

10

11

12

13

Illuminating Our Current Paths

Having peeked into our futures yesterday, let's take it one step further and do a meditation on our final outcome cards to help illuminate the outcomes of our current paths.

The tarot card in
   position 13 from the "A Future
   Forecast" spell (page 157)
Gold, yellow, or orange candle

Lighter or matches
Journal
Pen

1. Place the final outcome card from the tarot spread from yesterday on your altar at bedtime. Place the candle in front of the card.

2. Light the candle and turn off the lights in the room so that the only light source is the candle's flame.

3. Sit in a comfortable position in the room so that you are facing the light of the candle.

4. Close your eyes and take 10 breaths, inhaling deeply through your nose and exhaling slowly through your mouth. Holding the image of the light, feel yourself drift into a state of relaxation.

5. Reflect upon the reading from yesterday and the symbolism of your outcome card. Visualize yourself in the card and let your mind play freely in your meditative landscape.

6. End your meditation by taking another 10 deep, slow breaths, before opening your eyes when it feels right to do so.

7. Blow out the candle and write down any insights that came to you.

Get Motivated

Regardless of how simple or intricate a spell is, planning is one of the best ways to get motivated for our future goals. Today, we'll work some practical magic by creating action plans for our success.

Cinnamon or vanilla incense   **Journal or day planner**
Lighter or matches   **Pen**

1. Light a stick of cinnamon or vanilla incense.

2. Make a new entry in your journal or day planner to write down your goals.

3. Think about the different areas of your life that ultimately lead to your success and personal desires being achieved. Think about your mental and physical health, spirituality, relationships, career, and hobbies. Try to write at least three goals for each of these categories. Remember to keep goals and timelines realistic to make them achievable, and consider the reward of each outcome and how your life will be improved.

4. Grab your incense stick and trace a pentacle over the page to further seal it with your intention.

5. Reflect back on your goals regularly.

Authentici-Tea Spell

By being our true selves, we attract the appropriate people into our lives. Oranges and honey are particularly effective for attraction work, while cloves are helpful at promoting self-confidence. Let's combine them and create an authentici-tea!

Orange	**Mug**
Peeler	**Honey**
Small saucepan	**Spoon**
2 cups water	**Piece of paper**
3 to 4 cloves	**Pen**
Black tea bag	**Lighter or matches**
Colander or straining device	**Cauldron or fireproof dish**

1. Peel an orange. As you do, focus on what makes you genuinely happy.

2. Place the entire peel from the orange into a small saucepan with 2 cups of water and 3 to 4 cloves.

3. Bring the ingredients to a boil and reduce the heat to a simmer for 10 minutes.

4. Remove the saucepan from the heat and add a bag of black tea to the water. Let it steep for 5 to 10 minutes.

5. Use a colander or other straining device to pour the liquid into a mug.

6. Add a dollop of honey and stir with a spoon in a clockwise motion.

7. Enjoy drinking the tea while you write down on a piece of paper your personal truths—the things that make you who you are.

8. Splash some of the tea on the paper and let it dry.

9. Light the paper on fire and place it in your cauldron while proclaiming: "I call the authenticity in me to come forth and be set free."

BIRTHDAY MAGIC

Making a wish and blowing out candles on your birthday can be an effective way to manifest success. I love to eat a slice of cake at the exact time of my birth. If you don't know the exact time of your birth, use your intuition and do it whenever it feels right to you. You can use numerology to reduce the number of candles needed to a reasonable number. For example, if you are turning 25, break the age down into 2+5 which equals 7, and use 7 candles for your birthday magic spell. When you make your wish, visualize yourself actually attaining it. And with a strong yet slow blow, extinguish the candles, knowing that your breath is the fuel that mixes with the transformative element of fire, which is then carried by the smoke into the atmosphere to manifest. Finally, ground your energy by eating your cake slowly to savor all the sweetness.

Good Luck Charm Bag

Charm bags are used in a variety of folk magic practices; they contain a mixture of animal, mineral, and herbal ingredients that all align with a magical intent. Today, we'll construct one to use as a good luck charm.

Pen

1 bay leaf

1 (6-by-6-inch) piece of gold or orange fabric

1 High John the Conqueror root

1 vanilla bean

1 tumbled citrine

1 small chunk pyrite

3 pennies

Cinnamon oil

Cord

Horseshoe charm (optional)

1. Use your pen to write your name on one side of the bay leaf. On the other side draw a horseshoe, a symbol associated with luck.

2. Place the bay leaf in the center of the square cloth. Say the following while blowing lightly on the leaf: "Bay leaf, grant me luck in my endeavors."

3. Repeat step 2 with each of the remaining objects—the High John root, vanilla bean, citrine, pyrite, and pennies. For each item, blow lightly and repeat the charm, replacing "bay leaf" with the name of the object you are enchanting.

4. Add 3 drops of cinnamon oil on top of all the ingredients.

5. With one hand, fold each corner of the fabric in and hold it up. With your other hand, slide down the top of the fabric to secure the remaining objects inside.

6. Use the cord to tie 4 knots around the gathered ingredients to seal the bag. If using the horseshoe charm, slide it down one side of the cord and make another knot.

7. Carry the bag on you, in your bag, purse, or pocket.

8. "Feed" the bag regularly by applying 3 drops of cinnamon oil onto the cloth.

Money Tree Spell

Popular in feng shui practices, the money tree is a token of good fortune and luck. Today, we'll put a witchy spin on this positivity plant to intensify our prosperity and success.

Money tree
Gold pot (optional)
5 pennies (preferably
  found outside)
Hole puncher or
  alternative device

Faux money (prop money,
  Monopoly money, etc.)
Green ribbon
7 of coins or pentacles tarot
  card, or printed copy of it

1. Purchase a hearty money tree plant prior to this spell. If available, also purchase a gold-colored pot for it.

2. Place the 5 pennies in the dirt, creating a circle around the base of the money tree.

3. Punch a hole into the faux money and slide the green ribbon through it.

4. Tie a bow with the ribbon around the braided base of the tree. While tying the knot, visualize money coming to you and say: "With this knot, I draw money to me!"

5. Pick up your 7 of coins or pentacles card. Reflect on the imagery of the card, as it is known for representing patient planning that leads to well-earned investment. Tuck the card into the soil of the plant to further align it with the desired result of abundance.

6. Every time you water and care for the plant, repeat the charm, "With this knot I draw money to me!" and visualize yourself surrounded by abundance.

Rich Witch Oil

One simple way to attract prosperity to our lives is by mixing oil blends to dab on ourselves or other objects that we wish to imbue with richness. Here is a potent prosperity potion that can help attract wealth and monetary success.

Scissors

Faux money (prop money, Monopoly money, etc.)

1 (15-milliliter) rollerball bottle

Gold mica

10 drops neroli oil

10 drops orange oil

10 drops vanilla oil

5 drops sandalwood oil

1 drop cinnamon oil

Fractionated coconut oil

1. Cut a strip from the faux money and insert it into the dry and empty rollerball bottle.

2. Add a pinch of the gold mica to enhance attraction with a bit of shimmer.

3. Add 10 drops each of neroli, orange, and vanilla oils into the bottle, one by one.

4. Add 5 drops of sandalwood oil and 1 drop of cinnamon oil.

5. Top off the bottle with the fractionated coconut oil. Cap it and shake it vigorously.

6. Apply the oil to your inner wrists, behind your ears, and your clavicle whenever you need a punch of prosperity and success. Additionally, apply a drop to door handles, office cabinets, and any other item linked to your ability to become prosperous.

Prosperity Poppet

Poppets are dolls used in folk magic to draw energy into the persons with which they are aligned. Today, we'll witch-craft one out of homemade dough with the intention of drawing prosperity and success to us.

Saucepan

2 cups all-purpose flour

¾ cup iodized salt

4 teaspoons cream of tartar

2 cups water

2 tablespoons vegetable or coconut oil

Pen

Bay leaf

Pyrite crystal

Ground cinnamon

Dried orange peel

Body bits (hair, nail clippings, saliva, etc.)

3 drops rich witch oil (page 164)

1. In a saucepan, combine the flour, salt, and cream of tartar.

2. Add the water and vegetable or coconut oil.

3. Cook on medium heat, stirring occasionally, until the dough has thickened. Set the mixture aside to cool.

4. Use a pen to write "prosperity and abundance" on the bay leaf.

5. Place the pyrite crystal in the center of the leaf.

6. Once the dough has cooled, add the cinnamon, orange peel, body bits of your choosing, and rich witch oil. Knead the dough evenly with your hands to mix the ingredients. As you knead, visualize abundance, prosperity, and success manifesting in your life.

7. Shape your dough into a human form around the bay leaf and crystal. As you do, enchant it by saying: "I am you, and you are me. May I draw in prosperity."

8. Place the poppet on your altar as a symbol of prosperity and success.

Enchant Our Careers

Today, we'll do a spell to enchant our career paths and better draw success to our future goals and ambitions.

Computer and printer or
**   paper and pen**
Small bowl
Pinch dried basil

Pinch ground cinnamon
Pinch ground ginger
Lighter or matches
Cauldron or fireproof bowl

1. Update your resume to include prospective jobs or responsibilities that are in alignment with your goals. While doing this, think about where you want to be and what title and responsibilities you want to have.

2. Print out your updated resume. If you do not have access to a computer or printer, you can handwrite your resume out on blank paper.

3. Use a small bowl to mix together a pinch each of basil, cinnamon, and ginger—all powerful agents of stimulating confidence, prosperity, and success.

4. Fold your resume four times to represent stability.

5. Light one edge of the paper on fire and hold it until the fire begins to burn the paper rapidly.

6. Toss your flaming paper into the cauldron. While it burns, add your herbs to the fire while saying: "Sacred flame, I ask of thee to take my career and enhance thee. Herbs of success and prosperity, may my career grow to better assist me."

7. Let the paper and herbs cool to ash. Discard the remains outside.

Pure Potential

Reaching our potential comes down to examining our strengths, weaknesses, goals, and hobbies. This simple candle spell ignites our personal drive to reach our true potential.

Knife
Red chime candle
3 drops frankincense
   or sandalwood oil
Pinch gold mica
   powder (optional)
Lighter or matches

1. Use a knife to carve a spiral symbol (pictured on this page) into the wax of a red chime candle, which is used for courage and power. Spirals are a powerful symbol for movement and a representation of growth in life's journey.

2. Anoint the carving with 3 drops of frankincense or sandalwood oil to stimulate blessings.

3. Add a pinch of gold mica powder to the candle and rub it all over the candle. This will create an iridescent golden sheen.

4. Light the candle and say: "Sacred spiral, symbol of growth, help me reach my potential as I move forward on my path."

5. Focus firmly on the spiral symbol. Let the candle safely burn out under your supervision and move along knowing that you are on the path of pure potential.

Increase Opportunity

Today, we'll harness the powers of Jupiter—the planet of abundance, success, and expansion—to help create additional opportunities in our lives. The spell should be performed during the planetary hour of Jupiter. The following website lists these hours based on geographical location and time zone: Astrology.com.tr/planetary-hours.asp.

Knife
Green chime candle and holder
1 drop cinnamon oil
1 drop clove oil
1 drop nutmeg oil
1 drop sandalwood oil
Pinch gold mica
Lighter or matches

1. Carve the glyph for Jupiter (pictured on this page) into the candle.

2. Anoint the candle with 1 drop each of the cinnamon, clove, nutmeg, and sandalwood oils.

3. Sprinkle a pinch of gold mica onto the wax. Rub the powder all over the candle.

4. Light the wick and repeat these words: "Jupiter, great giant of our solar system, ruler of abundance and success, giver of expansion, I call upon thee to increase opportunity for me."

5. Let the candle burn through the hour of Jupiter.

6. Blow out the candle and repeat steps 4 and 5 during the planetary hour of Jupiter for the next day or two, until the candle has burnt completely down.

SIGIL MAGIC

Sigils are symbols that are created for a magical purpose and that hold a specific energy. The creation of sigils can be the magic itself, but sigils can also be used in combination with spells to strengthen their manifestation powers. Sigils may be drawn on petitions, carved into candles, or tattooed onto skin. There are many different ways to create sigils. Some use a wheel of the alphabet and trace the lines between letters to manifest their symbol. Others combine letters, and yet others use a combination of preexisting shapes collaged together into one. There is no right or wrong way to create sigils. What matters is the meaning behind them.

Personal Power Sigil

Today, we'll create our own unique sigils to manifest success in our lives. The process is simple and can greatly impact our personal magic.

Paper
Pencil

Candle, in the color of your intention (see page 36)
Lighter or matches

1. Determine what mantra best represents your personal power. It should be proactive and in the present tense. For example, it could be: "I am fabulous, successful, and free!" Use this example or write out another personal mantra on your piece of paper.

2. Cross out all the vowels of the sentence. In my example, this becomes MFBLSSCCSSFLNDFR.

3. Next, remove all duplicate consonants. The result of my example becomes MFBLSCNDR.

4. Begin sketching a symbol that combines all the letters of your remaining letters. My example is below.

5. Carve it into a candle in the color that is most directly aligned with your sigil's purpose. Light the candle and focus your energy on the intention behind the sigil. You can allow the candle to burn down completely, or burn it a little each day until it is gone. You can also add it to any object to further imbue it with your magical intent.

Magical Vision Board

The vision board is a tool to visually remind ourselves of goals while working toward manifesting them. When fueled with the intention of a witch, this fun and creative activity ultimately becomes a magical tool to further ignite one's destiny.

Magazines, newspapers, or
  other printed graphics
Photo of you
Scissors
Glue
Artboard, thick paper,
  or cardboard

Markers
Paint
Dried herbs or
  flowers (optional)

1. Gather several magazines, newspapers, or other photos that you can print to use.

2. Select an image of yourself to include in the project.

3. Cut out a variety of images, letters, and words that represent your goals.

4. Use glue to attach the images to an artboard, thick piece of paper, or cardboard.

5. Using markers or paint, draw designs, words, symbols, your power sigil, or anything else that inspires you. You may even wish to glue on some dried herbs or flowers.

6. Charge the completed vision board by stating: "With this perfect vision that I create, shall I manifest my perfect fate."

7. Hang the finished product in a place you frequently visit and take a moment each day to look at it.

Making Tracks

"Making tracks" refers to making forward progress. Our tracks are our footprints: what we leave behind as we progress. As we near the end of our self-care journey, let's unlock the doors to make tracks with wherever we're headed next.

Dirt from your footprint	**Gold or orange chime candle**
Plate	**Lighter or matches**
Knife	**Compass**

1. Go outside and find a place with exposed dirt. Step on the dirt hard enough to make a footprint. You can do this while wearing shoes or barefoot.

2. Collect the dirt from your footprint.

3. Spread out the collected dirt evenly onto a plate.

4. Carve your name into the candle. Lick your thumb and slide it over your carved name to seal it with your essence.

5. Place the candle in the center of the plate. Using the index finger of your dominant hand, trace a line through the dirt extending from the candle to the northern edge of the plate. Do this again for the southern edge, then the eastern edge, then the western edge. As you do, say: "From north to south, east to west, open the road for me that is best. With my tracks I push through to discover a journey that is brand-new."

6. Light the candle and gaze into the flame. Visualize new paths manifesting as you work through any obstacle that stands in your way.

7. Allow the candle to safely burn out. Use the remaining dirt to draw a line outside your front door so that your tracks cross over it each day moving forward.

A Self-Care Celebration

Congratulations, we've made it the 90th day of magical self-care! In honor of our success, let's have a ritual celebration to reflect on our achievement and realign with our initial dedication.

Musical playlist
1 fresh white rose
Lighter or matches
White candle
Remains from the white candle
  used in A Dedication to
  Self-Care (page 56)

Remains of spells
  you've performed
Printed photo from A
  Dedication to Self-Care
  (page 56)
Cauldron or fireproof bowl
Champagne or libation
  of choice

1. Prior to this celebration, create a playlist of 5 to 10 songs that make you feel happy.

2. Create a circle of rose petals large enough for you to move freely in.

3. Ground and center yourself.

4. Light the candle and thank the universe, any deities, ancestors, the elements, or other divine expression for their assistance and guidance. Speak freely from your heart.

5. Sprinkle any wax and other remains from your previous spells into the melting wax around the flame to symbolize the integration of your past, present, and future.

6. Place a corner of the photo into the candle's flame as an act of gratitude and symbolic gesture that you are no longer the person in that photo. You have evolved.

7. Toss your flaming photo into the cauldron and let it turn to ash. Dispose of the ashes outside after you complete the ritual.

8. Raise a glass to toast yourself. Eat, drink, dance, and be merry!

MOVING FORWARD

By using the spells, remedies, and rituals in this book, we have tapped into our need to live a more balanced life. How does it feel? Do you feel lighter? More energized? So now what? How do we move forward on our journeys?

Having established a magical mindset around daily self-care, we must continue to take time to reconnect with our minds, bodies, spirits, environments, and relationships to achieve personal success. The exercises in this book can be repeated. Writing our own spells based on the information in this book and the additional resources provided on the next page can also ensure that we keep self-care front and center.

Trust your intuition and adjust the spells according to your personal needs. Be patient with the process and continue learning. Always love yourself, honor yourself, and restore your energy so that you can be a powerful source of positivity in the world. Keep going and growing. The magic is in you, and you are magical.

Take care and make magic!
Michael

RESOURCES

The following is a full list of my recommended books, online resources, podcasts, and stores to continue your exploration of witchcraft and self-care.

BOOKS

The Art of Witch **by Fiona Horne** is a manifesto for living a healthy and spiritual life as a witch. A book that refrains from providing spells or using props, this is a great resource for learning how to care for yourself organically to live magically.

Light Magic for Dark Times **by Lisa Marie Basile** is filled with self-care goodies while also providing a variety of spells, rituals, and resourceful advice on how to light yourself up with magic.

The Modern Witch's Guide to Magickal Self-Care **by Tenae Stewart** explores using witchcraft and astrology to enhance self-love and self-care.

ONLINE RESOURCES

Witch Way Magazine (WitchWayMagazine.com) is a digital publication featuring curated articles about witch culture, craft, and daily life.

Witch With Me (WitchWithMe.com) is an online community for witches to further hone their craft.

PODCASTS

The Fat Feminist Witch Podcast is a fun and sassy podcast that examines witchcraft and spirituality from a feminist perspective.

The Witch Daily Show is a daily podcast that goes over headlines, books, topics, witch-fails, and more.

The Witchcast Presented is a bewitching podcast for dreamers, misfits, seekers, and believers hosted by internationally acclaimed witch Lucy Cavendish.

Each listed podcast is available on multiple online resources including iTunes and Spotify.

STORES

Bébé Vaudou (BebeVaudou.com) is owned by the immensely talented singer, songwriter, and witch Brooklynn and offers hand-crafted candles and magical supplies.

Hex (HexWitch.com) is a wonderful shop to stock up on all your witchy necessitates. It also hosts HexFest, an annual magical conference with presenters from around the world covering a wide array of topics for magical and spiritual practice.

REFERENCES

Basile, Lisa Marie. 2018. *Light Magic for Dark Times: More than 100 Spells, Rituals, and Practices for Coping in a Crisis*. Beverly, MA: Fair Winds Press.

Brown, Tonya A. 2019. *The Door to Witchcraft: A New Witch's Guide to History, Traditions, and Modern-Day Spells*. Emeryville, CA: Althea Press.

Conway, D. J. 1995. *Animal Magick: The Art of Recognizing and Working with Familiars*. St. Paul, MN: Llewellyn.

Cunningham, Scott. 1985. *Cunningham's Encyclopedia of Magical Herbs*. St. Paul, MN: Llewellyn.

Dombrowski, Kiki. 2017. *Eight Extraordinary Days: Celebrations, Mythology, Magic, and Divination for the Witches' Wheel of the Year*. Nashville, TN: Phoebe Publishing.

Grey, Peter. 2013. *Apocalyptic Witchcraft*. London: Scarlet Imprint.

Herkes, Michael. 2020. *The Complete Book of Moon Spells: Rituals, Practices, and Potions for Abundance*. Emeryville, CA: Rockridge Press.

Herkes, Michael. 2019. *The GLAM Witch: A Magical Manifesto of Empowerment with the Great Lilithian Arcane Mysteries*. Dallas, TX: Witch Way Publishing.

Herkes, Michael. 2020. "Spellcraft 101: How to Manifest Magic with Intention." *Diviner Magazine*, September 2020, 10–12.

Horne, Fiona. 2001. *Seven Days to a Magickal New You*. Thorsons.

Horne, Fiona. 2019. *The Art of Witch*. Summer Hill, New South Wales: Rockpool Publishing.

Horne, Fiona. 2000. *Witch: A Magickal Journey*. Thorsons.

Melody. 2003. *Love Is in the Earth: A Kaleidoscope of Crystals*. 3rd ed. Wheat Ridge, CO: Earth-Love.

Nertney, Bibiana. 2017. "The Importance of Self-Care." October 23, 2017. Accessed November 15, 2020. MyCPID.com/importance-self-care.

Rhea, Lady. 2019. *The Enchanted Formulary*. Scotts Valley, CA: CreateSpace.

Wigington, Patti. 2020. *Witchcraft for Healing: Radical Self-Care for Your Mind, Body, and Spirit*. Emeryville, CA: Rockridge Press.

GLOSSARY

anoint: To smear or rub oil onto yourself, a ritual item, or spell ingredient

aura: The energy field surrounding one's body

banishing: A form of magic used to expel negativity or unwanted energies

body bits: A collection of personal items such as nails, blood, and saliva used in spells to directly tie energy to you

chakra: Energy vortexes in the body that contribute to one's energetic vitality

charcoal disc: A block of charcoal used for burning powdered incense blends

charge/enchant: To imbue an object with energy

circle: An energetic boundary created to conduct rituals, ceremonies, or spellwork inside it

glyph: A magical symbol that represents zodiac signs, planets, asteroids, or other cosmic points

ground and center: Balancing emotional, mental, and physical energy into a state of peace

invoke: To call the energy of a deity or entity into yourself

libation: A beverage used in a ritual or spell

pentacle: The witch's symbol, a five-pointed star encased in a circle; each point represents one of the four elements (earth, air, fire, water) and spirit, and the circle around the star represents protection and the never-ending cycle of life, death, and rebirth

pentagram: A five-pointed star without a circle

petition: A magical writing that expresses the spell's need or desire

poppet: A magical doll used to align the magic with a specific person or self

shadow: An unknown side to one's personality that the conscious ego rejects, encompassing personality traits that have been suppressed, pushed away, and ignored, often as a result of the negative consequences associated with them

INDEX

ACKNOWLEDGMENTS

A huge thanks to Callisto Media and Rockridge Press for taking a chance on this book. Thank you to Vanessa Putt and Sean Newcott for your help in conjuring it into life.

To Amara Dulcis, for taking my bitterness and making it sweet. Thank you for all the late nights, crazy calls, being a shoulder to sob on, that 15-hour magical road trip we took while I wrote this book, and your selfless, unconditional friendship.

To Christina Harris, my best friend in the world and the butterfly who taught this caterpillar how to grow his "FABULOUS!" wings. Thank you for sharing your wonderful recipe with me.

To Yazmin Ramos, I love you to the moon and back. Thank you for being there through the writer's block and all our happy and sad times over the years.

To E. V. Heart and Jenni Love, the "Two Chicks Bewitched" who have bewitched my heart forever. Thank you for sharing your adaptation of the elderberry syrup.

To Fiona Horne and Tonya Brown, my ride or "flies" and sisters of magic, for your heartfelt advice, continued love, support, and guidance.

To Jesse Gillespie, my brother of magic, for sharing your wicked wisdom.

To Kiki Dombrowski, for your generous help with those eight extraordinary days.

I'd also like to thank my diverse group of friends and family who have continually contributed to my magical well-being: Kay Traylor, Kiara Lewis, Lynne Herkes, Mario Alequin, Silvester Padilla, Tania Drezek, Theresa Newton, and Valerie O'Connor. I love you all so much!

Also, a big thank you to the fabulous Kit Kat Lounge and Supper Club, particularly Mimi "Madam X" Monee, for the many opportunities, divaliciousness . . . and martinis!

And of course, thank YOU for reading this book.

Blessed be!

ABOUT THE AUTHOR

 **MICHAEL HERKES**, also known as "The Glam Witch," has been a practicing modern witch for more than 20 years. He is a devotee of the goddess Lilith and focuses his practice on crystals, glamour, love, moon, and sex magic. Michael is the author of *The GLAM Witch* and *The Complete Book of Moon Spells* and is a contributing writer and graphic designer for *Witch Way Magazine*, a digital publication featuring curated articles about witch culture, craft, and daily life. Additionally, Michael hosts the IGTV "Glam Fridays" on the Witch With Me IGTV channel @ witch.with.tv, offering tips and tricks for magical makeovers. He is a professional tarot reader and nationwide speaker, having presented at festivals such as Gather the Witches, HexFest, and WitchCon, in addition to being featured in an exhibit on display at the Buckland Museum of Witchcraft in Cleveland, Ohio. He lives in Chicago. For more information and to follow Michael online, visit **TheGlamWitch.com**.

CPSIA information can be obtained
at www.ICGtesting.com
Printed in the USA
JSHW011525260422
25199JS00001B/1